THE AMAZON SELLER CENTRAL SELLING GUIDE

Our Blueprint to Growing Your Seller Central Sales

AMZ Advisers

ABOUT AMZ ADVISERS

AMZ Advisers is a full-service eCommerce & digital marketing consultancy with extensive experience in creating high-growth strategies for brands and manufacturers on the Amazon platform. We partner with companies looking to realize their full eCommerce potential. In 2016, our partners enjoyed $20,000,000+ in sales with many of our partners experiencing more than 100% increase in their year-over-year sales on the Amazon platform.

We believe that developing a robust eCommerce presence is integral for a business looking to maximize growth in the 21st century. Our custom strategies aim to make Amazon, the largest eCommerce marketplace, a powerful sales channel and the centerpiece of every company's eCommerce presence. Long-term growth requires developing alternative sales channels, and we compliment every client's eCommerce strategy by bringing them to additional eCommerce platforms, developing powerful sales funnels and creating websites designed to convert shoppers into customers.

TABLE OF CONTENTS

INTRODUCTION

Amazon has continued to grow its shopper base by unprecedented rates and create incredible, new opportunities for businesses. The eCommerce retail giant has become the go-to starting point for customers searching to buy products online. Small businesses and multinational corporations alike stand to benefit massively from being on the platform. However, many are being left behind from not understanding how the platform works, not using the most cost-effective and efficient ways to grow on Amazon, or not having a presence on the platform at all. Our Amazon blueprint can help any business increase their sales and realize their full potential on this incredible platform.

This book is a culmination of our years of work on the Amazon platform. Through selling products ourselves and growing our clients' sales, we have discovered the most cost-effective and efficient ways to utilize the Amazon platform. Our failures and successes have guided us along the way to creating these powerful strategies. The focus of all our efforts has been to find the best ways to help our clients and to bring them the greatest value possible. We are proud that our custom strategies have helped our clients consistently hit goals and reach entirely new heights for their businesses.

In 2016, our clients broke the $20,000,000 mark for total sales on the Amazon platform. Considering total sales across all platforms, our clients achieved more than $33,000,000 in total sales. We love diving into a business and finding the best ways to grow their business quickly. Our clients averaged 67% growth over prior year sales and our largest clients achieved over 150% growth – some in as little as 5 months – during 2016. Our strategies are constantly evolving and we will continue to search for new growth avenues for our clients' products.

We've designed this book to be the ultimate reference guide for every person or business interested in growing their eCommerce sales. The book certainly can be read section by section, but is designed to provide valuable advice and insight into specific topics around the

Amazon platform. Feel free to read the entire book, or flip to sections that are relevant for the platform and stage that your business is at. These strategies work best for established businesses looking to scale, but implementing any of these strategies will take your business to the next level no matter where you currently are.

We hope that you take advantage of our tips and insights into the Amazon platform to realize your company's full eCommerce potential!

Part 1:
Selling on Amazon General Topics

THE AMAZON MARKETPLACE IN 2017

The Amazon marketplace took the eCommerce world by storm in 2016, and its upward trend is not likely to abate this year. Amazon has been pushing hard in the last decade, and has made impressive strides every year since its expansion from its humble beginnings as an online bookstore. This year, the dominant internet retailer is expected to extend its global reach, expand into physical shops around the US, and dive further into focused logistics, AI and entertainment efforts.

New Amazon Marketplace Options

As more and more sellers join the Amazon marketplace to enjoy low-risk eCommerce debuts and high-profit business expansion with this well-established platform, growth for the internet retailer is inevitable. Amazon completed a massive Prime Day promotion last year which pulled in record membership sign-ups and boosted mid-year sales. They have obviously been gearing up for a big year, in which seller expansion into new international markets plays a big part.

The US and Europe

For US sellers to be able to take their offerings to the world, Amazon opened avenues to over 70 countries. Amazon US sellers are also tapped into Canada and Mexico with the North American unified account option, and can enter the European market as well with the more recent European unified account. Europe is the second largest Amazon marketplace after the US, encompassing France, Germany, Italy, Spain, and the UK and representing a potential market of 300 million shoppers.

To attract more global sellers, the platform has been working on opening local sites in several countries. With these options looming large, now is the time for sellers to prepare to expand internationally to take advantage of this open road to success. A single account in one European country allows sellers to warehouse in this one location and take advantage of FBA services to cater to the entire European market.

China, India, and Beyond

Amazon has also launched efforts to enter China and India. China is proving to be difficult with strong local pressure against foreign companies, but the platform has succeeded in attracting a lot of Chinese sellers with their Dragon Boat program. Chinese merchants can easily move their inventory into FBA with special added privileges to help them along the way.

Struggles with Indian regulatory issues are also hindering the eCommerce giant's entry. Intensified efforts are working to grow that market, and this year may be the year that the Amazon marketplace breaks through. Amazon has invested heavily in India, and the company is poised to pour in another 3 billion US dollars to push its expansion there. The addition of Prime Video is only one of the perks that new subscription packages will include.

Australia could be the new Amazon marketplace of the year following the company's search there for warehouse space. Amazon already has one warehouse in Brazil, and this could be the next marketplace in line, despite barriers such as protective customs and high import duties.

Getting Physical

Amazon began as an online retailer to provide an alternative to traditional bookstores. The online giant has since evolved into a diverse marketplace, and is now back on the ground with their pioneering Amazon Go grocery. This 1,800 square foot swipe-and-go store is not your traditional brick and mortar shop, but offers a tech-aided shopping experience that does away with the need for dragging items to a cashier and standing in line to pay. Still a major retail opportunity, Business Insider reported that Amazon has plans of opening another 19 Go stores across the US in 2017 and 2018, plus perhaps as many as 2000 Amazon Fresh stores by 2027. Amazon books has also gone back to basics with the opening of four bookstores that feature test areas for their branded hardware like Kindle. This year will be the year this physical expansion truly takes off.

Logistics Takeover

Amazon has spent the last decade building a truly impressive logistics system. Billions of dollars go into shipping costs each quarter, and this number is continuously rising as the internet retailer drives to deliver faster and to more consumers. Their recent efforts to overtake courier services has led business analysts to believe that Amazon is planning a grand logistics takeover. Amazon is currently leasing trucks, planes, and ships, and has not given up on their drone delivery project.

Disruption Magazine says that Amazon is not only trying to manage all shipping internally, but attempting to launch an app resembling Uber to connect trucks and shippers. This would put Amazon in the running against Uber acquired trucking service Otto. Both companies plan to expand their offerings to shipping by sea and air. The plan would save Amazon over a billion dollars every year. Combined with Amazon's plans to open physical stores around the country, this massive shipping endeavor could also target other retailers in need of logistics services.

As the company takes care of more and more of its own door-to-door deliveries, shipping costs are bound to fall. The free shipping minimum on Amazon.com has already been inconspicuously lowered to 35 US dollars. As the system develops, Amazon's logistics app will integrate pricing, routes and stops while saving on third-part commissions.

Amazon AI

Amazon launched its nifty AI virtual assistant Alexa over two years ago, and its hardware counterpart Echo has been recently upgraded. Before Google and Apple even began with their own versions of this high-tech voice-controlled helper, Amazon was already working on its system to answer customer questions, order products and play music. To maintain its edge over the competition, Amazon has over 1000 people stepping up efforts to keep Alexa fresh, and get this proprietary AI into third-party devices such as the GE smart lamp. Tech Crunch reported in November last year that Amazon was ready to launch its AI platform to bring the technology to outside developers. There are currently three Amazon AI tools available – Rekognition, Amazon Polly, and Lex – but the company has definite plans of adding more over the next several years.

Media Changes

The Amazon marketplace has been offering video on demand since 2008, but has big plans of expanding its service by tripling its current library within the year. The online retail leader has been acquiring a large volume of original movies, TV series and documentaries in an apparent bid to compete with content streaming giants Netflix and Apple. Amazon began offering its video-only monthly subscription plan just last month, expanding the service outside of the Amazon Prime membership.

Amazon has made good on its announcement in November 2016 to implement changes in shipping rates, Buy Box eligibility and media fees by March 1st of this year. To start off, sellers in the media categories now have the freedom to set their own shipping rates by region and even offer free shipping for standard delivery. Sellers also enjoy the ability to compete for the Buy Box for all books sold in new condition. Finally, Amazon has changed the Variable Closing Fees to a fixed fee of 1.80 US dollars per item, and calculates the Referral fee based on the total sales price of an item rather than a percentage of its sales price These changes can push sales for new books up while evening up the competition with Amazon and publishers for the buy box, but used books sellers are going to face even tighter profit margins.

More Smiles All Around

All in all, things are looking up for Amazon and Amazon marketplace sellers this year. There are new avenues of opportunity that sellers can take hold of right away, and more to look forward to throughout the year. This expansion and the renewed focus on logistics also raises hopes that Amazon will be a stable platform on which to establish long-term business ventures. Sellers on and off the platform can also consider expanding from online sales to getting their products in Amazon Go stores at this early stage. Media retail might not be too hot, but lowered shipping fees could take the edge off. On the other hand, the competition generated by Amazon's video efforts is going to be great for content producers and consumers.

HOW TO RANK FOR KEYWORDS ON AMAZON

Every seller faces the challenge of getting their products ranking on Amazon. Identifying the main keywords that will convert is vital to sustained Amazon success. Ranking for those keywords is an entirely different battle. We've worked with some of the largest brands to optimize Amazon listings, develop, and implement strategies that will improve their Amazon ranking. Taking the steps below has worked for our clients and will help you rank for keywords on Amazon.

Creating SEO Copywriting for Your Listings

The first to step to rank for keywords on Amazon is to introduce keyword rich content into your Amazon product listings. Amazon's A9 algorithm tries to rank products by their relevancy for each keyword. Creating titles, bullet points and product descriptions that contain the most relevant keywords is the key to improve your Amazon ranking.

Start by researching the most relevant keywords to your products by using tools like Keyword Inspector or Google Keyword Planner. Keyword Inspector is a great tool you can use to crawl your competitors' listings to determine what keywords they are ranking for. It provides a detailed list of keywords that are in the listings and where they currently show up in search engine results pages (SERPs). Google Keyword Planner can also provide great keywords; however, the results are more focused on internet searches and contain keywords not necessarily relevant to a shopping platform like Amazon.

Develop titles, bullet points and product descriptions that use your competitors' top keywords. We recommend using the bullet points to focus on a product's benefits rather than their features. Focusing on product benefits shows shoppers how this product can benefit their lives and can be useful for converting them to customers. As you develop a sales history, Amazon will index you for these keywords on SERPs.

Ranking Products through Sales History

Having the right keywords is the first step to rank for keywords on Amazon. Developing the sales history will increase your visibility on SERPs. The A9 algorithm determines product relevancy by ordered units, conversion rates, click-through rates and product price. All these items are related and it can be difficult to separate how one change influences product rankings on Amazon. We first recommend picking a price that is below the average price of all the products on page 1 for the specific keyword you want to rank for and sticking with that price. Fixing this variable at a specific price will help you identify changes in the other metrics.

Now we can focus on improving the sales history. We recommend starting with discounted products to develop your sales history. Amazon's new seller terms of service indicate that giving products away for reviews is illegal. However, you still can offer discounts to drive traffic. Try creating a promotional discount that you believe will entice shoppers and market that offering through your social media channels or an email list. This can be done by sharing the offer with your current followers and/or, if you don't currently have much of a social media following, running advertisements on Facebook, Twitter and Instagram. Discounted sales still appear to hold equal weight to a full price sale and will begin to build your sales history.

Amazon should begin to index you for the main keywords in your content with these initial sales. The next step we recommend taking is to create automatic advertising campaigns on Amazon. Running these campaigns will make your products appear for the keywords in your listing as well as related keywords that shoppers may be searching for. This will lead to increased sales and provide you important feedback on what other keywords you should consider introducing into the front-end of your listing.

A final step that you can use to rank for keywords on Amazon would be to introduce manual advertising campaigns with Bid+ active. Bid+ is a feature that will increase the maximum cost per click (CPC) bid that are eligible to appear at the top of SERPs. The maximum increase is 50%. For example, say you are currently bidding $1 for a keyword and the top bidder is bidding $1.25. If you have Bid+ active, it will increase your bid up to a $1.50 CPC and your ad will be appearing at the top of the SERP versus your competitor's. Bid+ campaigns can be expensive to run, but are a great way to get conversions on the main keywords you are trying to rank for. Expect higher ACOS and a lower ROI from Bid+ campaigns, but the benefit will hopefully be increased organic sales as your product listing continues to be indexed by Amazon.

Resources

Google Keyword Planner
Free keyword research tool that can provide valuable insight to high traffic keywords on the Google Search Engine
www.adwords.google.com/KeywordPlanner

Keyword Inspector
A keyword research tool developed for Amazon sellers that focuses on finding the keywords that customers use while searching for a product or niche
www.keywordinspector.com

Sellics
A suite of tools that offers a free trial and is designed to help research keywords, optimize listings and grow your business
www.sellics.com

The 4 Amazon Product Ranking Algorithm Factors You Can Impact

Many sellers are feeling slighted by Amazon lately. Policy changes to the product review guidelines have changed strategies. Using discounted products to drive reviews and increase customer conversions are no longer possible. We've been saying since the change that the only way to be successful now is to increase your sales. Amazon is attempting to help with the reviews, but how can you as a seller increase your sales? One simple change that you need to test out can impact the Amazon product ranking algorithm in your favor. We are going to go through a case study of a few changes we made for a client and how it ranked them on Amazon.

The Most Important Factors

Amazon's A9 algorithm is governed by a few main rules and have a single goal in mind; to provide the most relevant results and best deals for their customers. The A9 algorithm only uses data on the Amazon database to determine product relevancy, and does not consider relevancy factors that search engines like Google look for (i.e., backlinks, off-page SEO). Amazon wants to maximize revenue per customer. It therefore tracks all customer data from what they search for to what products they click on after searching to what product they end up buying.

In our experience, there are 4 main factors that can increase product relevancy in the Amazon A9 algorithm. The most important factor is **sales history**. Amazon will index your product based on the search terms present in the listing and how many sales you get on each search term. Getting sales on search terms is a huge indication to Amazon that your product is relevant to the customers' search. It is important to optimize Amazon listings with search terms that are relevant to your product. Too often we see clients going after random keywords that are barely related to their product. Amazon will index for those random keywords and it ends up hurting the seller because the second factor is negatively impacted.

Conversion rates play a very important role in your product's ranking. Converting on a specific search term is another massive relevancy signal for the Amazon A9 algorithm. We've seen through our experience how conversion rates can help boost your product's visibility and we will share that with you. Therefore, focusing on keywords directly related to your product is incredibly important. You will end up killing your conversion rates by going after random keywords that are only slightly related to your product. Similarly, **click thru rate** is relevancy signal that Amazon values. Customer's clicking on your product listing shows product relevancy for the search term. While still important, we believe it is much more important to convert that click into a sale as much as possible.

The final factor is **pricing**, and it's the only factor that you can control. As we said, Amazon wants to show the most relevant results and best deals for the clients. We've noticed that pricing below market averages can give you a huge initial boost to your product. By testing out new pricing strategies you can impact the Amazon product ranking algorithm in your favor.

Case Study: Pricing's Impacts on a Product Listing

We recently worked with a client that launched a product in early January 2016. The product was launched at an above market average price. Initially, the product did not start moving until they dropped the price down a few weeks later. In the chart below you will notice that as they decreased price, page views, orders and conversions increased:

Case Study: Initial Launch

- ▶ Product initially launched at ~$23.00 with few units ordered
- ▶ As product price dropped - conversions, page views orders increased
- ▶ Price increased by middle of March to >$23.00
  - ▶ Conversions, page views and units ordered dropped off
- ▶ Analysis shows significant negative correlation between price and sessions, page views and conversion rates (r=-.63 to -.70)
- ▶ Regression analysis shows moderate relationship between price and performance (r² = -.5 for each independent variable)

These increases are directly related to the product becoming more visible on Amazon. Maintaining a consistent price continued to increase these factors. As the client began to run out of inventory, they started increasing price. The result was a drop in all 3 of those factors. The client killed their conversion rates by increasing the price and thus product visibility decreased drastically. The interesting thing is that even as they decreased price in the following months, product sales did not return. Correlation analysis shows a strong negative relationship between price and sessions, page views and conversion rates. Their relevancy suffered directly from the increase in price.

We began working with this client in late August. They had ordered a thousand units of inventory after their initial success and were now stuck with a product that wasn't moving. We overhauled the product to create an optimized Amazon listing. Low relevancy keywords were removed. Then we began testing new pricing points to see how the product performed. As the product crossed the $10 per unit threshold there was a massive up-tick in conversion rates, orders and page views:

Case Study: Product Re-Launch

- Began working with client in late August
- Introduced SEO content into listing and began testing new price points
- Below $10 per unit conversion rates, orders and page views jump
- Metrics fall again when price is increased above the $10 per unit threshold
- Correlation analysis shows strong negative correlation between price and sessions, page views, units ordered and conversion rates (r=-.73 to -.83)
- Regression analysis shows strong relationship between price and conversion rate (r² =

The inventory began flying off the shelf and thus the product relevancy was confirmed in Amazon's eyes again. Conversion rates reached as high 50% and page views increased by ~700%. The client was achieving success similar to their initial launch. We attempted to increase the price slightly over time and these metrics began decreasing again. The correlation analysis again showed a strong negative relationship between price and conversion rates, orders and page views. The client had achieved page one visibility, but was doing it a reduced profit in exchange for higher volume. Dropping pricing can be a powerful, yet tricky tool to impact the Amazon product ranking algorithm.

What Does All That Mean?

Pricing will directly impact your visibility within the Amazon product ranking algorithm. More importantly, **it shows that you need to differentiate your product**. This client was in a highly competitive market with a product that was just like everything else on the market. The private labeled item had no unique value proposition to customers and could only compete on price. We're now working with the client to improve their offering and achieve higher profits in the future.

Anyone could implement these same strategies to begin dominating a market. Downward pricing pressure from competitors will kill your product on Amazon. When choosing a product to sell, look for opportunities to differentiate yourself through bundling with a complimentary product or possibly working with your manufacturers to design unique features. Amazon is a great sales channel, but it's also extremely important to grow your product outside of the Amazon platform.

Utilize effective pricing on Amazon to get your product moving initially. Be willing to break even on your sales for as long as possible to develop the sales history that you need. Having a high-quality product and high volume of sales will lead to increased product reviews (or social proof) that will highlight your quality in shoppers' eyes. Do not drastically increase price to prevent selling out your inventory. This will kill your listing's relevancy within the Amazon product ranking algorithm. Slowly test increased pricing over time and check the sales data to see the impact it has on your listing. A differentiated product that has a unique value proposition to a client will be able to be priced higher without product relevancy being impacted as drastically.

7 Tips to Increase Your Amazon Sales

The question posed by many Amazon sellers is how to increase sales on the Amazon marketplace. Amazon is the largest and fastest growing ecommerce platform today and poses incredible opportunities for established businesses and startups. As opposed to search engines such as Google and Bing, Amazon users are potential customers looking to buy. The key to success on the platform is product visibility. This can be achieved in a few different ways. We've developed these ideas for selling on Amazon through our extensive client work. Check out our tips and tricks for selling on Amazon to learn how!

1. **Listing Optimization:** The Amazon search algorithm is designed to show customers the most relevant listings to their queries. It bases the relevancy on the keywords used throughout your product listing. Boosting sales on Amazon starts with the copywriting in your front end. It's important for two reasons: keyword relevancy; and, converting customers. Amazon crawls your listing's title, bullet points and product description for keywords and partly uses these to index your listing. It's important to have keyword rich content – but avoid keyword stuffing as the algorithm will recognize too much density as an attempt to manipulate the algorithm. This is against the TOS. Your listing also must convert page visitors so it's important to call out the features that make your product beneficial. Use the bullet points to highlight features and increase conversion rates.

2. **Backend Optimization:** It is also important to optimize the backend of your listing. The more information you provide to Amazon will help you index for the product better. One area

to utilize fully is the search term area. Amazon currently allows 1000 characters (including spaces) in each search term field. Use phrases and long tail keywords that customers could be searching for to find your product. To test if you are indexed for the search terms, copy and paste any random section. Search in Amazon and you should see your product come up within 24 hours.

3. **Advertising Campaigns:** Utilizing Amazon Sponsored Ads as a seller is an important part of how to increase sales on the Amazon marketplace. Showing up on page one is the goal of every seller. While it can happen right off the bat, chances are your product will not appear on the top pages. Running advertising campaigns is key to boosting sales on Amazon and moving up the search results pages. Run automatic campaigns to collect keyword ideas to use in your campaigns. Collect the data over a few weeks. Use the data from the reports to improve your backend search terms, listing page and build manual advertising campaigns. Bid higher on the manual advertising campaigns and let low bid automatic campaigns capture sales from keywords you may have missed. This can help you increase Amazon sales rank of your product by placing your product on the first page in the form of an advertisement.

4. **Product Promotions:** Utilizing the product promotions and giveaways features of seller central are great ideas for selling on Amazon. Enticing sellers to purchase your product through a discount can get you the momentum you need for boosting sales on Amazon. Amazon changed their review policy preventing sellers from providing discounts in exchange for reviews. Many sellers believe these reviews are how to increase sales on the Amazon marketplace. While reviews are important, the sales from these discounted purchases is what will increase Amazon sales rank and product visibility. You can publish discount codes directly on your listing or create a

promo codes that can be used in offsite marketing campaigns.

5. **Off-Platform Advertising:** One of the most important, yet least used tips and tricks is to advertise outside of the Amazon platform. Running social media ads can be a great way to build buzz for your product and generate sales. Utilize promotional codes to entice potential customers to learn more. Direct customers to a landing page where they can put in their email and receive the promo code. This allows you to build a customer list for future marketing and a better audience for your online advertising campaigns. This is how to increase sales on the Amazon marketplace in a major way!

6. **Selling Internationally:** Moving into international Amazon markets is another great way how to increase sales on the Amazon marketplace. The biggest markets outside of the US currently are Canada, the UK and Germany. The sales volume is smaller in these countries; however, the competition is also very low. Getting into a market early can position your product for long term sales. Utilizing Fulfillment by Amazon is the same as in the US. Each market has different tax requirements that you will need to consider. Soon you will be asking how to increase sales on Amazon UK!

7. **Product Price Point:** The price point of your product could be holding you back. Amazon tends to feature lower priced products toward the top of their pages. We've seen what simply dropping the price can do for boosting sales on Amazon. A recent client of ours dropped their price and went from no visibility to the 2nd page. The lower price will increase Amazon sales rank through additional sales. This can help you move up the rankings in extremely competitive markets. Make sure you have enough inventory before dropping the price too much or you could run out quickly!

This has only been a brief overview on how you can increase your Amazon sales. We've tested these ideas and many others with the clients we have worked with and seen incredible success. We believe that implementing these steps will help you increase your sales and improve your best seller ranking.

Leveraging Facebook Ads for Amazon Listings

Facebook ads is one of the channels that holds great promise for increasing conversions. Facebook is the biggest and fastest growing social media platform in the world. No other social media network can compare to its features, and most of all, its audience. Facebook has 1.86 billion monthly active users as of the fourth quarter of 2016. This is billions of potential customers for anyone with something to sell on Amazon. Facebook advertising is in constant revision, and it has grown to provide a wide array of features for advertisers. Sellers know that there will never be enough marketing channels, and Facebook ads is not one to miss.

Facebook Ads Capabilities

Facebook ads allows advertisers to target specific audiences and market products and services to them easily and effectively. Many sellers from Amazon FBA eCommerce retailers to big brands have been using Facebook ads to drive record sales and grow their businesses. Facebook has proven time and again to produce a very high ROI for many sellers. Some sellers have been so successful marketing with Facebook ads that they have recovered their ad spend by as much as 700%. Well-optimized campaigns have brought in so many new customers that Facebook has come to account for as much as 70% of sales for some businesses.

Facebook Ad Targeting

Facebook has exceptionally accurate targeting capabilities. The company has developed this mechanism over the years through data collection, analysis and improvements on their algorithms. By efficiently targeting billions of global users, Facebook presents a very attractive ad package. Through Facebook ads, sellers can identify and target specific audience segments for different products or for the same products at different times.

Ease of Use

The Facebook ad platform has been designed to be very easy to use. Even sellers with not a lot of experience on the platform or with ads themselves can navigate their ad accounts with relative ease. There are also many help resources available to provide support for getting started with audience searches and ad campaigns.

Organic Amazon Boost

Facebook is extremely effective at increasing sales. Amazon sellers can therefore experience organic ranking boosts for listings that receive traffic from Facebook ads. Organic rankings on Amazon are strictly monitored, so a true organic boost for any product is priceless. Sellers who direct traffic through ads with a good conversion rate will gain a valuable edge over the competition in the long run.

Getting Started

To begin using Facebook ads to boost your business sales, you will need to set up a business page and an ad account. Below we outline the simple steps that you will need to go through to prepare for your first Facebook ad campaign.

Your Facebook Business Page

1. Go to your Facebook Business account and click on the drop-down at the top right corner. Click on Create a Page.

2. From the available options, select the page category that best suits your business. Brand or Product is often the best choice for Amazon sellers.

3. Next, select your industry-specific category, and enter your basic business information in the spaces provided.

4. Review your selection and entries and Agree to Facebook Pages terms and conditions when you are satisfied.

5. Click Get Started to launch your new business page.

6. Optimize your page by adding a concise and interesting description of your brand, a link to your Amazon page or your eCommerce website, and your logo as your profile picture.

7. Selest the option to reach more people to get more visitors to look at your page.

Your Facebook Ad Account

1. Open the Facebook Ads Manager and navigate to the Settings on the left side of the page.

2. Enter an account name, your business time zone, and your industry.

3. Select the option for using Facebook ads for business.

4. Carefully enter the additional required business information, review and finish.

5. Upload your product catalog to your account, including product names, images, pricing and other product details.

Install Conversion Tracking Pixel

The pixel is a code snippet that enables you to track visits, conversions and ROI from your Facebook ad account. The pixel also enables Facebook to use the tracking data to optimize your campaigns and build lookalike audiences to help you target better.

Once you have uploaded your catalog to your Business account, make sure that you add a custom audience pixel and set it to give you reports on your customers' buying behavior. This will help you identify site visitors for retargeting. Facebook needs time to gather data, so consider running your first ad campaign at least one month after your pixel is set up.

Lookalike Audiences

Facebook can use the data it has collected to help you to find new customers as well. Based on the demographics, characteristics and interests of past customers, Facebook can suggest Lookalike Audiences that you can advertise to. These audiences will have similar characteristics and therefore likely be interested in your products. Lookalike Audiences are a very high performing target group.

To create a Lookalike Audience, you first need a Custom Audience. You can build one from your Facebook Fans or data from your pixel.

Facebook Ad Types

Facebook ads in general are known to do wonders to increase traffic and conversions. There are, however, certain ad types that have proven more effective. Below we introduce the features of these Facebook ads to give you an overview of what you can expect.

Dynamic Product Ads

Dynamic product ads are possibly the highest ROI strategy. They are useful for regaining the interest of customers who are on the fence. These tailored Facebook ads can be targeted to specific customers based on their previous activity on your site. Amazon itself along with other eCommerce sites use Facebook retargeting to offer site visitors discounts and other enticements for recently viewed products.

Dynamic Product Ads feature prepared templates that pull the product names, images, pricing and other information straight from your product catalog. Whatever product details you have uploaded to Facebook Business Manager will be automatically reflected on the ad. This is especially useful for sellers with many products to manage.

All you need to launch a Dynamic Facebook ad is an ad title, your product names from the catalog, and keywords to find the right images. Then choose if you want to advertise products from your entire catalog or only specific categories. You can also display single or multi-product ads to your site visitors, regardless of what stage they reached.

Multi-Product Ads

Multi-product ads show multiple products to your audience in a single ad. This provides options for customers that you feel have not clicked buy or processed their carts because they are still looking around. With more choices, they are more likely to find what they want and complete their purchase. Multi-product ads can also be used to present the different features of one product or to test images for your listing by monitoring your click-through-rate. Cost per click also decreases over time as more people engage with the ads.

When using Multi-product ads separately from Dynamic Facebook campaigns, navigate to the Power Editor to begin setting up a stand-alone ad.

Run General Retargeting Campaigns

Abandoned carts is a huge eCommerce problem. As many as 70% of your customers may fail to complete their purchases. In addition, only 8% of them are likely to some back later. When you properly retarget these shoppers, you can encourage as many as 26% of them to come back to complete their orders. Retargeted ads in general have a click-through-rate that is ten times higher than regular ads.

To start running retargeting campaigns, navigate to the Power Editor to set up audiences and design your offers, upload coupons, or create single and multi-product ads.

Bonus Features

You can also use a series of Facebook ads to tell your brand story and to connect and build relationship with prospective and current customers. Short videos with a valuable message also communicate well and are well received even by people with limited time. With Custom Audiences, you can also create unique lists of people from emails or phone numbers. This way, you can reach out to your customers and encourage them to become your Facebook fans. Keep in mind that those customers who are great at sharing your posts should be rewarded with special offers and other perks.

FINDING THE TARGET AUDIENCE FOR YOUR AMAZON PRODUCTS WITH FACEBOOK ADS

Utilizing Facebook ads to drive traffic to your Shopify store or Amazon listings is a powerful way to increase your products sales. The key to a successful, or cost effective, Facebook advertising campaign is to find your target audience – the consumers most likely to purchase your product. Running broad Facebook advertising campaigns will lead to higher cost per click (CPC) and will reach too many people who will never actually purchase your product. We're going to discuss ways to find the target audience for your Amazon products and how to refine that audience to maximize the return on investment from your advertising campaigns.

How to use Facebook Audience Insights to Your Advantage

Every Facebook Ads account has the Audience Insights page that is a powerful way to find the target audience for your Amazon products. You can look at audiences by location, age, gender and interests among many other factors. As you filter down through those factors, Audience insights will provide demographic information, the pages the like, their locations, online activity and purchasing behavior. We can use this information to begin creating a target audience for our products.

This is a great place to begin identifying your target audience. You will need to continually refine the audience by utilizing the Facebook Pixel. The pixel is installed on a landing page or in your Shopify store to gather information on the shoppers that click-through your advertisements on Facebook. You cannot, however, use a pixel if your ad is direct linking to your Amazon listings. Therefore, we recommend using a landing page service like ClickFunnels or AMZ Promoter if your goal is to increase sales on Amazon. Both services allow you to integrate the Facebook Pixel with your landing page.

2 Ways to Find the Target Audience for Your Amazon Products

The first step in finding your target audience will be to begin searching by interests. For this example, we will assume we are selling a camping product to illustrate how we choose the audience more effectively. We will search "Camping" in the interest field and check out the size of the overall audience. Audience Insights say that this interest has 10-15 million monthly active people on Facebook, which is a large audience. We are going to refine this audience down, but we typically want interest audiences that have 250,000+ monthly active users.

Next, we are going to look at the top 10 "Page Likes" for people in this interest category. We want to see how related the top page likes are to camping. Click through each page that comes up in the Top Categories section to see what these pages are related too. We typically look for about 80% or more of the pages to be related to camping. After we go through that, we are going to repeat that process by typing each page into the "Interests" search by itself to see how related those audiences are to camping. Not all pages will come up which typically means their audience is too small and Facebook does not have enough data on them. Exclude those pages from our list. Spend a good amount of time identifying pages and products that are related to your product.

Now we are going to break these pages into a few segments so that we can begin testing what segment has the best conversion rate. There are 4 main segments we look at. The first would be influencers or personas associated with the interest. These typically have dedicated fan bases that may be passionate about the product category. Next, we would look for information websites or pages that provide help or tips in this category. These audiences are actively seeking information on how to do or use something so there is a strong likelihood that they currently consume similar or related products. We are then going to look at publications or magazine pages, particularly those that have subscription services. People interested in these pages may own subscriptions to the publication and therefore have already purchased something in this category. Finally, we are going to look for product, program or service pages related to the interests. Like the prior category, these people have a higher likelihood of buying something in this category.

Set up the split test by creating 4 ad sets under 1 campaign – with each ad set focused on one of segments. We recommend setting a small daily budget of $5 or so per ad set so you do not blow through money. Install the Facebook pixel into your landing page to track the click-thru rate. You may see positive results that point to one segment being better than the others in as soon as 1 day.

Another way to identify the target audience will be through cross-referencing, or flex-targeting, pages and targeting high affinity pages. What do we mean by this? Facebook Ads give you the ability to refine audiences by page like. So, to cross-reference a camping interest we may enter the "Camping" interest into an ad and find an audience who likes camping and likes a related camping page we are cross-referencing it with. This leads to smaller, more targeted audiences. We split test that against the page affinities. Audience Insights also provides data on page affinities, which means the likelihood that the audience is going to engage with the content. Targeting high affinity pages can target people that are very interested in the category, and may also get us some free advertising if they share or like your content.

Take the list of pages that you have already researched and find their monthly audience numbers and affinity scores on the "Page Likes" section of Audience insights. Create a campaign and then create an ad set that we can use the cross-reference strategy on. Type in the main category interest into the "Detailed Targeting" section, so in this case Camping. Below that field, you will notice a link to "Narrow Audience" appears. Select it, and then begin typing in an interest to see how it affects the audience size. The goal is to get an audience size between about 75,000-500,000. You can do that by entering multiple requirements into the first "Narrow Audience" field – or by adding additional cross-references by selecting "Narrow Further." Once we reach the ideal audience size, we will have a very focused audience to begin split testing with.

We will begin split testing the audience in the above paragraph against an audience of high affinity pages. Look at the list of page affinities and find what the average affinity is. Take those pages with the above average affinity scores for our comparison audience. We will then set up the campaign with two ad sets – one testing the cross-reference segment versus the affinity segment. Set the budgets for each segment at about $5 per day. Make sure your ad is going to a landing page with the Facebook Pixel installed to track your click-thru rates.

There is no easy way to track actual conversions if your traffic is being direct to Amazon. You are not able to install the Facebook Pixel onto page listings. One thing you could do to see conversions coming through Facebook ads would be to create a unique promo code for a small percentage off that you use exclusively to market your content in the Facebook ad. You can then go back through your orders and see what orders had this code applied. It won't be specific to which ad set got the sale, but as you begin narrowing by pausing ad sets you can gain a better idea by seeing if your conversions increase or decrease with each change.

It's important to find the target audience for your Amazon Products to increase your products sales. Directing traffic through Facebook to your listings can be a great way to build your sales history and boost the product up the page rankings. These two strategies have led to increased sales for our clients and can do the same for you. You can also implement these same audience targeting strategies to drive traffic to Shopify, BigCommerce or WooCommerce stores as well!

CREATING A SALES FUNNEL FOR AMAZON

Marketing campaigns through Amazon can drive additional traffic to your listings and hopefully increase conversions. A more powerful way to advertise your product on Amazon – or any ecommerce platform for that matter – would be to create a sales funnel. Being 100% reliant on the Amazon platform for sales is not a winning strategy and can set you up for hardship in the future. By creating a sales funnel for Amazon, you can find potentially interested customers to purchase your product and continue to target them in the future.

What is a Sales Funnel?

A sales funnel is what many ecommerce companies and service oriented companies use to attract potential customers and turn them into consumers. Many companies use the image of an upside-down pyramid separated into different parts to represent it. The top of the upside-down pyramid (essentially the base) is all your marketing efforts to find potential customers that may be interested in your product. As customers enter the funnel they are funneled into the middle of the pyramid where the sales process occurs. This is where the customer learns more about your product and decides if this is something that will make their life easier or better. Finally, at the bottom of the upside-down pyramid, you have your customers who decided to purchase.

Why are Sales Funnels Important?

Sales funnels are important as they provide a few different benefits to a seller. One of the benefits is that a sales funnel can be used to drive traffic to your listing. The depth of many of the categories on Amazon can make it very difficult for your product to show up on search results pages, particularly in competitive markets. Utilizing a sales funnel strategy can be a great way to get your product in front of potential customers, start converting sales and move up the Amazon rankings organically.

Another great benefit of a sales funnel is building a target audience. A good sales funnel allows a seller to collect email addresses of their potential customers through an opt-in page. You can use these emails to create target audiences on many advertising platforms and find more potential customers. The emails can also be used in email marketing campaigns to let customers know of new products you may be rolling out, discounts you are offering or possibly to retarget them for the original product.

How to Create a Sales Funnel?

The most effective way to create a sales funnel is through utilizing social media advertising. Use social media platforms to market to potential customers and to grow your product or brand awareness. Make sure your advertisement has some benefit to the potential customer that will entice them to click. As potential customers begin to click on your advertisement they will need to be redirected to an email opt-in page. Many social media platforms will not allow you to link directly to Amazon and will need to go through a landing page or your website first. Once they opt-in to receive the benefit that was advertised to them, they can be redirected to learn more about the product or redirected to the Amazon page to purchase the product.

Utilizing Social Media Influencer Marketing

Influencer marketing is not at all a new marketing strategy, but the tactic has gained traction quite rapidly on social media in the last year or so. The words of public figures go a long way in boosting recognition for products and services. And what better way to get those recommendations out today than via social channels? Savvy consumers tend to steer clear of advertising because they no longer trust these types of messages. A thumbs up from a renowned celebrity appearing in their feed, however, will be paid due attention.

Two things combine to make influencer marketing a powerhouse strategy. First, no form of advertising can yet compete with word of mouth. Second, social media is where everyone is these days. Therefore, leveraging social media influencer marketing can increase brand awareness and raise conversion rates by as much as 50%. Once your influencer marketing campaign is off the ground, word is also likely to spread even further as other fans share the posted recommendations. That's free marketing right there, which can give your sales another boost. In 2016, social media influencer marketing became an established form of promotion. In 2017, it is set to blast through the roof with 50% of brands signifying intent to dive into influencer marketing campaigns.

Influencer Marketing Explained

Influencer marketing is a strategy that relies on the popularity and authority of a known figure in a certain industry. A social influencer is an authoritative figure who has gained standing in social circles. There are many such online celebrities who have gained a solid following and actively engage fans on different topics. They do not necessarily give full product endorsements or testimonials about specific services, but may work in mentions from time to time in their daily updates. Being an influencer is linked to a certain charisma, and people flock to such magnets and almost cling to their every word.

More than just gaining exposure, influencer marketing gets your product or service in front of targeted audiences and associated with the big names that will draw conversions. It isn't the type of direct advertising that has become such a huge turn off. It is the guy next door's favorite online talent just sharing his thoughts on this or that with everyone tuning in to see what he has to say. Consumer reviews have already proven to be a huge factor in purchasing decisions, and having an influencer leave a similar comment on any one of the many popular networks is a powerful thing.

Putting good money into influencer marketing may seem like a frivolous investment at first glance. Interests shift fast and social media trends follow. Influencers know this, however, and so fiercely guard their audiences. They want to make sure that they never sell out because they know that as soon as they let their genuine voice slip away, their fans will quickly follow. They must keep the experience organic to survive, and brands can ride this trend for as long as the world appreciates authenticity.

Integrating Influencer Marketing

Influencer marketing is, simply put, finding the right pull for your push and investing in getting those mentions for your brand. You can get started on making it an integral part of your marketing with the following steps.

Set Goals Aligned with Your Brand Image and Larger Strategy

Every successful brand has a closely guarded image and well-maintained message. Set your goals for your influencer marketing campaign so that they flow seamlessly with your content strategy and positively build your brand's reputation. Influencers can help boost product launches, generate hype for events, create and promote new content, and turn bad PR around. If you are working in any of these areas in your current strategy, you can begin your search for the right influencer to carry it out.

Identify and Locate Your Influencer

The best social influencer for your specific goals will have a sizable audience composed of the perfect set of individuals for your offerings and the level of credibility that you need to achieve your targets. Your influencer will have an authentic voice that supports your image and evidently attracts and keeps the attention of your target market. He or she will also have a consistent presence on the best channels for your desired audience. You will be able to see and feel how much trust the audience places in your prospective influencer, and gauge the potential impact from there.

To find such influencers, you will need to get on social networks and do an active search. There are a few types of software available that can make the search easier, but a manual search will allow you to follow leads that a machine would miss and to get a real feel of how your prospects move within their spheres of influence. Remember that influencer marketing revolves around word of mouth, so when you find one or two that you like, ask them to point out a few others who might work for your campaign as well.

Make Contact and Offer Value

When it is time to reach out to social influencers to form relationships, you should always make direct contact. Using an agency might take less of your time, but this is part of that old advertising system that influencers and their followers stay far away from. Get in touch directly to show your sincerity. Just as you would with a fresh sales lead, be honest and personable, avoiding the sales talk and focusing more on learning about them. From there, you can learn what drives them to do what they do, and be able to offer them real value in exchange for their help.

Keep Track of Progress

Influencer marketing falls within the realm of native advertising, but this organic approach can still be monitored. Even if you are just using a simple spreadsheet to take note of posts and updates about your brand and offerings, you can keep an eye on what is happening and how it is helping you reach the goals that you have set.

Take It a Step Further

Once you have formed stable relationships with key influencers, you can level-up your influencer marketing campaign by inviting them to post on your social channels. This will firm up the connection between the authority and your brand. It will also help you gain more followers on your business accounts.

Act Fast!

Since influencer marketing is still a relatively open area as businesses continue to test the waters, you can make a big splash and net a good number of big fish for a small fee if you act quickly and start making influencer marketing part of your marketing strategy today. Influencer marketing is has not reached its saturation point yet, but marketers are catching on and companies will soon be competing for the best names to speak for their brands. Now is the time to get in the game and capture these powerful movers before they establish ties with the competition.

Search Engine Optimization for Amazon Mobile Shoppers

Mobile shopping is on the rise and is predicted to double in four short years. The problem is that the mobile experience is horribly lacking, particularly around optimization. Buyers spend 20% more-time shopping via mobile devices, but end up spending only a sixth of what they do on desktops. Many are abandoning their carts in frustration because mobile commerce should be more convenient, but just doesn't offer the same quality results. Sellers and brands who fail to create an optimized mobile shopping experience are losing as much as a 65% increase in sales.

The good news for Amazon vendors is that the fully optimized Amazon app is drawing these shoppers away from other stores who are unprepared to offer the best mobile experience. This means that the market is ready, but the question is whether vendors are set to receive the incoming flood of around half of all mobile shoppers. Many vendors have become quite adept at optimizing their listings for e-commerce desktop users, and it is now time to get started on perfecting these listings for m-commerce.

The Mobile Experience

One of the key elements in optimizing Amazon listing content for mobile users is consideration for the mobile experience. Basically, mobile devices have smaller screens, and mobile users have less time. These two main points affect m-commerce in very similar ways. For instance, it is tiresome to try to read through long descriptions on a mobile device, and mobile users are usually on the go, and cannot spare the extra few minutes that it would take to get through a listing to find what they are looking for. Because these users are normally busy doing something else while browsing, they are more likely to select a product that can show them the most important information upfront. An optimized m-commerce Amazon listing therefore presents clear and concise information that these users can easily accommodate.

Optimizing for Mobile

Keywords

Keywords are still a very important component of your m-commerce listing text. The Amazon App search feature uses them in much the same way as the desktop version does to identify the closest matching products. The trick here is to add your relevant keywords in a shorter format. It may be tempting to use all the available characters, but this can dilute your content and bore your typical mobile shopper.

You should look for a balance here:

1. Focus on the main key words and phrases that rank the highest for searches.

2. Incorporate another one or two in a straightforward description of your product's main benefits.

3. Incorporate another one or two in your best use cases.

4. Incorporate another one or two in your best examples.

5. Incorporate one or two in a tagline, or a summarized version of your brand mission.

This is a basic suggestion, but you should feel free to play around with the text to get the most coherent and complete whole. The elements can be combined in your five sentences as you see fit to aid in emphasizing your product's best features and strongest selling points.

Titles

Your product titles will render differently on mobile than they do on desktop. Most often, titles will be shortened to save space, so you will need to arrange your titles so that the most important words are at the beginning. These can be your best keywords, or your brand name if it is a popularly searched term. Coherence is better than cramming, so you should develop short phrases of four words on average and separate these with commas so that readers won't get confused.

Writing Copy

Once you have your sentences with keywords, it is important to check for readability. Pay close attention to the proper placement of these keywords so that they aid comprehension rather than cloud it. Next, make sure that the text flows together nicely from one point to the next so that they can get all the information effortlessly. You want them to be able to skim through at least this first and most essential part of your listing. If the text is disorganized or distracting, mobile users will rarely take a second look to understand it better, and will leave without the great takeaway that will hook them into buying from you.

Formatting Text

There are two main sections in an Amazon listing, the Features and Details and the Product Description. The first section is where you should separate your five content elements above into bullet points. This makes it easier for the mobile reader to take in small chunks of information at a time, facilitating faster comprehension. Bolding, italicizing, and using all caps for the most important words and phrases further enhances your customers' experience.

The Description will most often not be read by mobile shoppers. However, if you could capture their attention above, they may decide to read on. This usually means that they are serious about making a purchase. To keep them keen on your product, it is best to use the same formatting strategy in your Description so that readers can still skim through to pick up the salient points. Since this section will have much longer text than above, use line breaks to separate your paragraphs. This works in the same way as using bullet points in the above. Saving one format type, such as all caps, for prefacing points will also help mobile users to absorb your content more easily to keep them interested for the close.

TIPS & TRICKS FOR SELLING INTERNATIONALLY WITH AMAZON

Making the decision to begin selling internationally can be daunting. Enthusiasm can be dampened by the anxiety that often goes along with the prospect of going global. Sellers must weigh various considerations before launching a global expansion. Accurate timing for the move is essential to getting good results faster, and rolling out to the global market with a full appreciation of the risks and costs is crucial to business success.

The Right Time to Go Global

If you have been thinking about whether you should start offering your brands and products to overseas markets, one or more of the following situations may have prompted you to start planning:

- Stagnant or scant growth in your current market and the need to reach additional markets to meet sales targets; or, great success in your current market, suggesting that it makes sense to move to the next level

- The promise of increased profits based on advantageous logistics in markets closer to the manufacturing source

- Inquiries from shoppers located outside your current market, indicating or supporting an impression that your brands and products would fill a need and be in high demand in other markets

Every business must be able to adapt to the market and seize opportunities for growth. With Amazon, the marketplace is no longer limited to Amazon.com and its linked markets in Canada and Mexico. Amazon

Europe offers five additional sites that can service a very large market comprised of nearly thirty countries in the European Union, and Amazon Asia offers three sites in the key countries of Japan, China and India that are poised to take the continent by storm in the next few years.

Amazon has strategically expanded to make selling internationally more attractive. They have taken advantage of the international markets that hold the top eCommerce promise. Joining Amazon at these hot global spots grants you entry to millions of new potential customers without having to start from scratch with the additional investments normally associated with a new location. Moreover, you can begin enjoying immediate returns because Amazon has already built trust with these shoppers.

Recognizing the Challenges

Having an amazing marketplace laid out before you is tempting; however, there are still several concerns involved in global expansion. Below are some of these considerations that must be carefully contemplated before delving into selling internationally.

Marketing Challenges

- Creating local awareness, such as starting fresh with no reviews

- Pricing adjustments to compensate for different costs and market tolerance

- Import restrictions

- Promotional timing, knowledge of local exposure points

- Product variety

Merchandising Challenges

- Changes in packaging and completing product information for compliance

- Compliance with regulations (both US and new market) such as privacy and security

Business and Financial Challenges

- Creating a local entity

- Credit-card fraud

- Additional costs for compliance testing, and for taxes, duties and customs fees

- Currency conversions, local banking and credit card processing

Operational Challenges

- Updating SKUs and translating listings for compliance

- Logistics issues such as shipping delays and fulfillment options

- Package inclusions

Customer Service Challenges

- Language barrier

- Customer service hours

- Managing returns

Technology Challenges

- Updating checkout fields and calculating additional fees

- Multicurrency pricing and multilingual views

Tips on Selling Internationally

Going global with your brands and products is a long-term commitment that will require a certain level of energy and financial support.

1. *Quantify your Marketing Resources* – Do you have what it takes to back up your global expansion over a period of three, five, or even ten years?

2. *Commit to the Long-Term Process of Going Global* – Are you prepared to begin the process of properly marketing your products to and streamlining your service process for a new market? Do you have substantial knowledge of the market to adjust your expectations and generate significant demand?

3. *Get to Know the Culture* – Are you familiar with different aspects of the buying culture, such as payment preferences?

4. *Research Your Sales Channels* – What have you learned about the general eCommerce atmosphere in your proposed new target market? Are you familiar with options within that area that are outside of Amazon?

5. *Familiarize Yourself with Additional Duties, Taxes, Import Fees and Customs Brokerage* – Do you know how to compute for customs fees? Are you familiar with VAT? Are you aware of the associated penalties for non-compliance? Do you know what you need to get your EORI? Is your accountant prepared to handle sales in different international jurisdictions?

6. *Lay out a Plan for Logistics Changes* – Do you have a plan in place for handling warehousing? Returns? Additional shipping stops for FBA preparation?

This list is by no means exhaustive, but a sampling of the different obstacles that you must prepare for before you can start safely selling internationally on the Amazon marketplace, or on other channels. Take the time to go through all the different nuances of selling in each of your prospective marketplaces. You may find that some of the locations that you wanted to enter look more manageable or more profitable than at first glance. If you have taken in all that needs to be done for a successful entry as an international seller, have all the resources to do what it takes, and are still excited about launching an expansion, then the time is right for you to start selling internationally.

SELLING ON AMAZON'S OTHER WEBSITES

Selling on Amazon is rewarding enough, but it became more enticing when Amazon acquired the very popular daily deal site Woot in 2010. This is not the only subsidiary that they own, however. The top destination for online shoppers is not called the online retail giant for nothing. Below we have an overview of the biggest of the websites and companies under the Amazon banner: online retailers Shopbop and Zappos, self-publishing platform CreateSpace, video streaming service Twitch.tv, audio bookstore Audible, audio book publisher Brilliance Audio, rare bookstore AbeBooks, gaming studio Double Helix Games, and maritime forwarding business Beijing Century Joyo Courier Service. Selling on Amazon now has new meaning with these and other avenues for online retail.

Shopbop – 2006

This online retailer has expanded its services since it was acquired by Amazon. Already trusted with a global customer base, Shopbop continues to sell high quality authentic designer merchandise for women. The site boasts a wide range of hand-picked apparel and accessories from fashion's current labels. Shopbop is known for its superb personalized customer service, which includes wardrobe advice. The site also offers front-line editorial lookbooks and select partnerships with future-focused brands.

Zappos – 2009

This online retailer is one of the largest online shoe stores in the world. The idea behind the company was to build a website that offered a large, high quality assortment of shoes. Zappos now also offers the best selection of clothing, accessories, bags, boutique, and various other items for men, women and children. The Zappos goal is to give the best service online in any category with a focus on fast shipping. The continuing goal of Zappos is to get customers to associate the Zappos brand with the absolute best service.

CreateSpace – 2005

This self-publishing platform is the result of a merging of two companies that Amazon acquired in the same year, CustomFlix and Book-Surge. CreateSpace offers self-publishing to authors, independent filmmakers and musicians. Subscribers can publish their own original works and easily distribute them through an on-demand system. The company offers these independents an innovative way to market their work to a wide audience while maintaining a good deal of control over the material.

Twitch.tv – 2014

This live video streaming platform focuses on live streams. Most content consists of video gaming, including competitive gaming event coverage, playthroughs of video games, multiplayer gaming, and broadcasts of eSports competitions. Twitch boasts a subscriber base of 100 million monthly visitors who have access to video material from 1.5 million broadcasters.

Audible – 2008

This audio bookstore focuses on the production and sale of audio entertainment, but also deals in online educational and information programs. Audible stocks audiobooks, audio versions of magazines and newspapers, and radio and TV programs. Since the acquisition, Audible has assimilated about five thousand Audio GO titles. Possibly Amazon's most recognized subsidiary, Audible is the biggest name in audiobook production and retail in the United States.

Brilliance Audio – 2007

This company is the leading independent US audiobook publisher. Brilliance Audio maintains a very high standard of audiobook publishing. They were producing audio copies of bestselling books at affordable prices long before the term audiobook was coined. The company is in a great position to compete for top fiction and nonfiction works of all genres with their reputation and fully equipped manufacturing facilities, studios, art department and global sales team. Brilliance Audio pursues its motto of "Audiobooks for Everyone" with more than 6500 titles to date on CD, MP3-CD, and for download, and offers volume publishing for certain print publishers.

AbeBooks – 2008

This book company works with independent bookstores to track down rare, used and out-of-print books. They pride themselves in a sizeable inventory of rare titles made available in over fifty countries and from thousands of booksellers. AbeBooks has six websites for France, Germany, Italy, Spain, North America, and the United Kingdom.

Double Helix Games – 2014

This gaming studio, famous for the games "Killer Instinct" and "Silent Hill", has more than a hundred game developers working on new games. The company hosts frequent studio events and focuses on maintaining an atmosphere that is most conducive to creativity and excellence. Double Helix Games is the result of a merger of The Collective and Shiny Entertainment; both Foundation 9 studios. The company is now one of the largest and most experienced in game development worldwide. They are also one of the developers of major home consoles.

BONUS for Selling on Amazon: Beijing Century Joyo Courier Service – 2016

This maritime forwarding business is part of Amazon's major drive to expand their logistics strategy to sea freight. Amazon has begun posting its rates for this new service, ready to compete with experienced global freight companies in China. Amazon's application for a license was approved by the US Federal Maritime Commission in early 2016, and the company is now pushing forward with its plans to operate as a non-vessel operating common carrier (NVOCC). Beijing Century Joyo has already run 150 containers of cargo shipment to and from China and the US. This may bring additional benefits to selling on Amazon for Chinese manufacturers. As Chinese shippers take this more affordable and direct option, savings are likely to filter down and make selling on Amazon an even more lucrative business.

Selling on Amazon's Deal Site Woot

Aside from the Amazon marketplace in North America, Europe and Asia, this mega company holds several other subsidiaries. A few of these are eCommerce sites, and the biggest of these smaller companies include online retailers Shopbop and Zappos, self-publishing platform CreateSpace, video streaming service Twitch.tv, audio bookstore Audible, audio book publisher Brilliance Audio, rare bookstore AbeBooks, gaming studio Double Helix Games, and maritime forwarding business Beijing Century Joyo Courier Service. Perhaps the most notable of these subsidiaries is Woot, known as the original daily-deal site. Below, we give you an introduction to Woot's sales model, marketing style, and a guide to begin selling on the site.

The Woot Sales Model

Woot is an online retailer popular for its main theme of offering different discounted products every day. The company's tagline is, unsurprisingly, "One Day, One Deal". The main website originally offered only one discounted product each day. The item would never be announced in advance, but it was usually electronics or computer hardware. The item would sell until it was sold out, and the next item would generally not be offered until midnight. After being acquired by Amazon.com in 2010, Woot began offering a new item if the day's item sold out before noon.

Other Woot sites offer daily deals for t-shirts, children's items, wine, household goods, tools, fashion accessories, sports equipment and other various items. Only the t-shirts were originally shipped outside of the United States, with all other items sent courier for a fixed fee regardless of weight or size. Since the acquisition, Woot is tied into the Amazon distribution network. Some shipping delays are still experienced since some items that are sold are not actually in stock. Woot customers can grab a limited number of deal items, sometimes one and a maximum of three. Some Woot deals are on refurbished items, which has caused data leaks on at least one occasion.

The one-deal-a-day Woot business model means that replacements are not offered for defective products. Customers can only request refunds, and customer support is non-existent. Woot customers are referred to the manufacturer or the user community on the Woot forums to file complaints or get information.

The Woot Marketing Style

Woot is a fun site that leverages humor to sell products. Product descriptions are strange and even crazy, often mocking not only the product but also the customer and Woot itself. Descriptions also straightforwardly acknowledge product downsides. The serious details of the products are also available, however, below the Woot description. Advice from the Woot community is also readily available through the forums, which function much like Amazon reviews in guiding would-be buyers. The forum is kept lively by various contests that are more for enjoyment than prize value.

Woot Benefits

The self-proclaimed primary benefit of selling on Woot is their honed mechanism for running flash deals. As the website Vendor FAQ explains, they are a good way to dispose of excess inventory, even items that would seem difficult to sell off. Woot agrees to take item quantities upfront, and pays vendors when the orders for the deal items have shipped out.

Woot will also take practically any kind of item. Vendors are welcome to send in their best offers to be evaluated by the team, who will then offer suggestions and a customized plan to suit vendor needs, such as disposing of unwanted items or testing the salability of a new product. Woot also offers several deal formats, such as featured daily deals, extended flash sales and the classic Woot-off sale that can extend the daily deal for a certain item to three days.

Vendors can take advantage of the Woot community as well as the sales members who often post detailed information about certain products and which features make them sell better. The marketing model is also a unique and powerful attraction factor.

Selling on Woot

To start selling on Woot, there is an onboarding process that is similar to becoming a vendor on Amazon. Prospective vendors will need to agree to the shipping and vendor terms, and submit a W9 to their assigned vendor manager. Successfully onboarded vendors can then start submitting deals and can expect to launch a deal within a month from that date.

Woot vendors will need to go through the SellerCloud integration process, which includes manual order import and tracking export. Vendors who have integrated a website that is not on the Magento platform will need to create a separate company for Woot orders to distinguish them from other orders made on the website. Inventory is not updated from SellerCloud with inventory feeds, however, so creating shadows is not necessary.

Plugins are available to facilitate the process. These plugins are placed on the vendor's server. Note that files must be imported manually since Woot does not support FTP access. Vendors can customize plugins to suit their needs, but different rates may apply for these changes. SellerCloud Support can provide details on the available plugin versions and customizations.

Order Imports

The SellerCloud Support plugin to take care of order import permits the direct import of Woot generated files. Customization includes importing orders as wholesale. To import an order, go to Import Orders under the Order menu and choose the company you want to transact with. Choose the option to use Website as the Channel and choose the Woot plugin from the dropdown. Select the order file that you want to upload from your computer and press the Import button.

Tracking Export

To export Woot-ready shipping confirmations, you can use the tracking export plugin. Go to Manage Orders and select the orders in question. Go to the action Menu and choose Export Orders, then press Go or the export icon located at the top right of the grid. Choose the Woot tracking export plugin and click the Export button. The task will be queued and the download will be available once completed, ready for upload to Woot. Shipped Woot orders can also be scheduled to export, along with other recurring tasks.

Maximizing Your Google Shopping Sales Channel

Google Shopping has a lot to offer online businesses. Some optimization is needed, however, for the platform to be effective. If you want to take advantage of this opportunity for growth, read on to learn about structuring campaigns and adjusting your shopping feed. Google Shopping can be a boon to your eCommerce store if you can invest some time into getting it set up to maximize potential revenue.

Mobile Influence

The world's shoppers are using mobile more and more. Over half off all Google Shopping clicks are from mobile devices. Just two years ago, mobile only accounted for about 20% of all clicks on the platform. It is due to this rapid increase in shopping click volume that Google Shopping ads are now filling the top half of the first page of Google's search engine results on mobile devices. Organic rankings and text ads are no longer visible.

To make the most of your Google Shopping campaigns, you need to keep abreast of these mobile trends. If you are getting half of your hits from mobile shoppers, then you need to do all that you can to ensure the success of your mobile campaigns rather than leaving mobile conversions to chance. Because of the very high volume of mobile traffic that we are seeing in general, and the continuing upward trend over the past two years, mobile is the future.

It is necessary for businesses to create both a mobile and a desktop strategy - possibly with a heavier focus on mobile advertising campaigns going forward. This thrust will require that you tweak the default settings in Google Shopping. The recommended settings are not going to get you anywhere near the level of profits that you could be raking in if you were to customize your campaigns.

Separate Mobile Campaigns

Because mobile shopping covered such a small margin until the massive surge between 2015 and 2016, most businesses did not bother to use the mobile targeting options that were available. Now, however, ignoring this market would be a grave error in judgment. Fortunately, AdWords is undergoing an overhaul. At first, there was no way to set Google Shopping campaigns to target different device types. Businesses could still tweak settings specifically for mobile to adjust bids and fine-tune ad settings, but the options are limited. Upcoming changes due to launch this year will make mobile targeting for each campaign even better with specific settings for desktop, tablets, and mobiles.

Mobile campaigns used to consist of dummy bids based on the desktop campaigns, which were simply a certain percentage of the desktop bids. This was the only way that the platform would be able to distinguish whether each click was for desktop or for mobile traffic. Google Shopping will soon allow businesses to create separate campaigns that give business owners complete control over all aspects of a campaign.

For advertising strategies that warrant separate campaigns to properly target desktop versus mobile users, this is great news. Business owners should be aware, however, that not all businesses need to make the additional investment to manage separate mobile and desktop strategies. The option is there, however, to use when a business sees a significant increase in mobile traffic.

Campaign Structure

The way that you structure your campaigns is going to have a big impact on how they perform. Take advantage of the different options that you have on Google Shopping to optimize your audience targeting, bids and feed. This way, you will be able to spend less and get better results faster.

Geographic and Demographic Targeting

A few tweaks for geographic and demographic targeting can refine your campaigns to make sure that your ad investment is well spent. The early stages of your campaigns are the research phase, when you should be gathering a lot of data so you can use it to make good decisions regarding your campaigns.

The Google Shopping default location is the entire United States. While this may seem like a good way to reach a wider audience, it is impractical. Businesses will usually get much more hits from certain states as compared to others. Targeting the whole country does not make good business sense. By learning which areas are bringing in the highest conversions, you can refine your geographic targeting and see an immediate increase in your ROI.

Demographic targeting options are not available by default on Google Shopping, so business owners must manually turn them on. To test the waters, you can add target groups to a campaign without setting bids and allow them to collect information before you begin spending on ads. You can also take advantage of demographic targeting to see even more data on who is showing interest in a product and who is buying it. You can also check socio-economic levels to see which areas have the extra income that makes shoppers more likely to seriously consider purchasing your products.

Custom Labels

Without custom labels, you will not be able to segment your ads to target different groups for specific products. Once you have collected a significant amount of information on your ideal audience, you will want to streamline your campaigns. You can save a lot of ad capital and put it to better use by serving ads for different products only to those who are most likely to be interested in and able to make a purchase. An additional advantage of custom labels is the ability to make separate bids for different products depending on which ones are the better sellers, which ones bring in higher profits for your business, which ones are currently available, on sale, and so on.

Shopping Feed

The way that a product is displayed is just as important to your potential profits as the quality of the product itself. Online shopping is highly competitive because of the much wider range of products available as compare to brick and mortar stores. You need to make sure that your shopping feed is the best that it can be to make your products stand out.

The attention span of the average customer today is shorter than ever before. Most people will give a single product a few short seconds before passing it over. You may still be able to sell some product without optimizing your feed, but you will lose out on a lot of sales. If you can capture the attention of today's ultra-impatient shopper, you may be able to improve your sales drastically. Learn how to show shoppers what they want to see and deliver it in a format that takes as little time as possible to absorb. Then you can win them over and maximize the resources that you have put into Google Shopping.

It today's market, good enough is never good enough. Businesses must utilize every platform available and provide high quality products to shoppers to grow. Your potential customers are not looking for something that is good enough. You must offer them something extraordinary. Anything less is a huge waste of time and ad capital.

Part 2:
Amazon Seller Central

Getting into eCommerce for the First Time

Ecommerce. One of the top catch-phrases of the internet era. Most people hear this term and think that they could never do it. Or it takes too much time. Or whatever their excuse may be. I'm here to tell you that ecommerce is easy and anyone can start making boatloads of money through the internet today. The opportunity is almost unlimited. Taking action does not need to be some incredibly over-the-top business plan requiring you to drive massive amount of traffic to your website. You can become an ecommerce professional today and start making money quickly by following the simple plan outlined in this book. I'm talking about selling a private label brand on Amazon

Many businesses have started out by selling on Amazon and you can do the same. Our goal is to help our readers achieve success on Amazon and we will be teaching you exactly how you can make money by selling on Amazon. But, before we get there... why Amazon?

Amazon Market Size

The most rapidly growing eCommerce platform by far is Amazon. com. Amazon has grown into an ecommerce marketplace where millions of shoppers can buy from an almost unlimited number of merchants. Amazon.com, and its foreign websites, present entrepreneurs and businesses with an incredible opportunity to reach massive audiences. And the number of users will only continue to grow.

In April 2014, Amazon had 244 million active users. Amazon Prime, Amazon's $99 per year customer loyalty program, had 54 million users as of January 2016 – a 35% increase from the same time last year. It's estimated that 44% of buyers now use Amazon as their primary search engine for finding products in place of traditional search engines like Google and Bing. And while Amazon in the USA is by far the largest Amazon marketplace, they continue to expand internationally and have a presence in 13 other countries. What does all this mean???

You're missing a massive opportunity if you are not selling your products on Amazon!!!

Selling on Amazon

There is lot of flexibility for businesses to sell their products. Amazon provides different options for merchants to sell on the platform; each with its own pros and cons. The first is the traditional *Fulfillment by Merchant* where orders come into Amazon, the retailer receives the order and ships out the product to the customer. This is how orders would be fulfilled on eBay or on a company website. The pros of this model are that Amazon charges a flat referral fee and does not collect additional fees. The cons are that this leaves the retailer responsible for shipping, returns and customer service – a daunting task for entrepreneurs starting out.

The next selling option is to utilize *Fulfillment by Amazon (FBA)*. In this business model the retailer ships their goods to one of numerous Amazon warehouses across the country and Amazon takes it from there. What does that mean? Well, it means that Amazon will handle all the customer service and logistics for the seller. This allows the retailer to focus on other aspects of growing their business! The downside is that Amazon takes more fees for doing all the work, but a sale is a sale and 1000s of merchants are currently using this platform to make massive amounts of monthly revenue.

The last option is more for established businesses, but it can certainly be obtainable for the right entrepreneur trying to scale their business in the future. Why do I say future? Because *Amazon Vendor Central* is an invitation-only program where you sell your products directly to Amazon and they handle the rest. The program essentially changes you from a retailer to a wholesaler or distributed and has tons of benefits!

Getting Started

What do you need to get started selling on Amazon? It's as simple as creating an Amazon account. Once you have an account you can choose to sign up to sell items on Amazon. You can then choose between signing up as professional seller or an individual seller. The decision really depends on the volume you expect to be doing. But if you are truly trying to start a business or scale an existing business, it makes all the sense in the world to sign up as a professional seller.

Resources

Amazon Seller Sign Up
www.amazon.com

Jungle Scout
A powerful research tool that extrapolates Amazon marketplace data to provide insights into monthly sales, revenue and best seller rankings based on keyword searches
www.junglescout.com

AMZ Tracker
A suite of tools to help you research products, track competitors and optimize your listings
www.amztracker.com

Sellics
A suite of tools to make managing your Amazon account easier
www.sellics.com

THE BUSINESS OF SELLING ON AMAZON

Amazon provides one of the most unique opportunities to grow a business that can generate long term profits. Selling on Amazon provides incredible opportunities for first time entrepreneurs and seasoned businesses to tap a massive market. The potential for your business is almost unlimited!

It is important that you know how an Amazon business functions. Here we will discuss the *Fulfillment by Amazon* and *Fulfillment by Merchant* business models, the successful selling strategies, and the Amazon business life-cycle.

Choosing Your Business Model

We briefly touched upon the two primary Amazon business models. A new seller on Amazon can choose to use *Fulfillment by Amazon (FBA)* or what we call *Fulfillment by Merchant (FBM)*. Each model has its pros and cons, but how do you determine whether FBA or FBM is right for you?

The answer to that question will be different for every seller. There are a few factors that you should consider when choosing your fulfillment model:

- How much time you want to spend on the business

- The volume of sales you expect

- Logistics

- Storage

- Customer service

Let's explore how these factors play into the FBM model. As a FBM seller, you will be posting your items for sale directly on Amazon. You will receive a notification in your seller central account every time you get a sale on Amazon. The notification will appear under "Your Orders" in the "Unshipped" row on the left side of the Seller Central Dashboard. You then need to ship out the products to your customers. How do the previously mentioned factors come into play?

FBM involves more time on the part of the seller. For each order, you will need to print out the packing slip, package the product and arrange for your delivery service to ship the product. This may not be an issue for low volume products, but some sellers may not want to do this for 10-20+ products a day. You also need to think about the size of your product and where you are going to store it. Unless you make the product yourself as orders come in, there will be boxes of inventory sitting around your house. Finally, anytime there is a complaint or a customer wants to return a product you need to handle that yourself. This may not be a viable option for a first-time entrepreneur.

FBA is way more hands-off and could be the right option for a first-time business owner or established business. You will post your products for sale on Amazon and ship your products to a Fulfillment Center. Amazon handles almost everything after that. They will package your product, ship it and handle returns. You may still receive messages from customers with question that you will need to respond to. But that is it. The time spent on the business is drastically reduced, volume isn't an issue (except for having enough inventory), and the logistics, storage and customer service handle themselves. It is almost a passive income stream.

Your margins selling with FBA are lower as Amazon takes fees for doing all the additional work. But the time you save could be well worth the added cost.

Common Selling Strategies

There are 3 common selling strategies that sellers employ on Amazon: *retail arbitrage; selling generic products; and, private labeling.* Anyone can easily replicate any of these strategies however we would recommend starting with the easiest one. This will help you get your feet wet and learn the ins and outs of Amazon.

Retail arbitrage (RA) is the simplest way to get started selling on Amazon. RA is taking advantage of pricing differences between brick and mortar retailers and the Amazon platform. It is essentially "buy low, sell high." Amazon has made it extremely easy for sellers to utilize RA. Once you have created your Seller account, download the *Amazon Seller* app from Amazon. This app allows you to view your sales, inventory and messages among other things. The feature that is used for RA is "Scan." You can scan any UPC barcode with the app and if the product is on Amazon it will show you what its Best Seller Rank is and where it is currently priced. Hit your local discount stores or big-box retailers (Walmart, Target, etc.) and start checking out the clearance section. You will be surprised at the selling opportunities you can find there.

An intermediate strategy is to sell generic products. This could involve selling anything from an unbranded pasta strainer to a shoe insert. With this strategy, you source your products from a manufacturer, wholesaler or distributor and list them directly on Amazon. Check if the product is already on Amazon by searching for the UPC code. Ideally the product is not on Amazon and you are the only seller of the product. If the product is already on Amazon, you may sell the product on that existing listing if it is an exact match and the listing is not restricted by Amazon. You would need to be the lowest priced seller, or win the buy box, for your inventory to move. This can drive prices way down on a product and make it difficult to be successful long term.

The best way to be successful long term on Amazon is by private labeling your products. It is like the above strategy in that you will be sourcing from a manufacturer. The distinct difference is that you will have the manufacturer place your logo (that you design) directly on the product or packaging. Branding your product gives you more protection from other sellers selling on your product listing. This allows you to consistently have the "buy box" and ensure your product is being sold. Private labeling has slightly higher start-up costs; however, the costs are well worth the return.

An Amazon Business Life-Cycle

This mostly applies to entrepreneurs that choose the private labeling strategy on Amazon. I want to briefly mention the steps to running an Amazon business. The start of any private labeling is researching the product that you want to sell. You need to choose a product and category that you can easily compete in. This will involve studying trends, the competition and paid advertising.

From there, you need to find a manufacturer to source your product from. You will need to speak to multiple manufacturers and get samples of each product from them. You want to make sure that your manufacturer produces a good quality product, is easy to communicate with and most importantly is trust worthy. The manufacturer may have the product in stock and can quickly apply your brand to it, but I would not expect that. More than likely the product will need to be made from scratch. Always try to negotiate the details with your manufacturer to avoid any confusion or frustration in the future.

The order will be placed and then you want to focus on creating the listing on Amazon. You will make the listing stand out by including SEO content, images and calls to action. The product will also need to have UPC codes to be sold on Amazon. These codes do not necessarily need to be on the product; however, it does make them significantly easier to get into inventory. Have the completed order sent to you so you can review the inventory and ensure it meets the standards that were discussed with the manufacturer.

The listing will then go live when you send the inventory to Amazon (if you choose FBA) or when you update the available quantity on the listing (if you choose FBM). The rest of your time will be spent creating paid advertising campaigns, improving your listings, responding to customers' questions and promoting your products.

THE NEW AMAZON REVIEW POLICY AND HOW IT AFFECTS SELLERS

On October 3[rd, 2016] Amazon updated their community guidelines related to incentivized amazon reviews. The new policy indicates that reviewers cannot not leave product reviews for any products that were received at a discount unless it was through the Amazon Vine Program or Kindle Direct Publishing. Amazon has revised their policy a few times over the past year and this latest policy change has a significant impact on the Amazon platform. **We are going to look at the reasons behind Amazon's updated reviewer guidelines, how the new Amazon review policy effects small sellers, and how to get Amazon customer reviews after this policy change.**

Why did Amazon update the policy and ban discounted product reviews?

Amazon has made a few updates to their review policy this year. This first change originally required sellers to have an account history of purchases totaling greater than $5. They then updated that threshold to $50 at the beginning of September. Amazon restricted the "Verified Review" badge to purchases with less than a 50% discount. Amazon also brought legal action against fake reviewers online over the past year. These policy changes are in-line with Amazon's legal action against fake reviewers. The legal action combined with the thresholds were intended to prevent individuals from providing fake product reviews. Unscrupulous sellers were using fake reviews to boost the appearance of quality of their products and to hurt competitors in the same market.

The most recent policy change is something that we believed was coming. Amazon faces a slight image problem that was brought to light by Birkenstock's decision to leave the platform. Counterfeit goods and poor product quality plague certain categories on Amazon. They are taking active steps to clean up the platform by banning discounted product reviews. We are also seeing Amazon deleting customer reviews that were previously left on a discounted product. Amazon's goal is that this will allow the best products to rise to the top by removing reviews that artificially made products appear better than they were.

How the new Amazon review policy effects small sellers?

The new amazon review policy effects small sellers disproportionately on Amazon. Discounted product reviews were a primary way that small sellers gain credibility among customers. Amazon deleting customer reviews and preventing discounted product reviews puts these sellers at a disadvantage. Small sellers now face more obstacles to increase their product's social proof without incentivized Amazon reviews. What we expect to happen will be that sellers launching new products or getting into selling on Amazon for the first time will have increased difficulty in driving organic sales. Reviews play an important role in converting shoppers into customers. We believe that without reviews small sellers will face lower ROI on higher advertising costs as clicks may lead to less conversions. Lower conversion rates will also have a negative effective on ranking for keywords.

The sellers that really benefit from this change are established sellers, who may have more money to implement other review strategies, and Amazon. The new Amazon review policy effects larger sellers less as they have larger budgets to spend on advertising or other methods that may get them reviews. Amazon already has strong review follow up campaigns via email that will drive organic reviews. This certainly favors products sold by Amazon and may push their listings further up search engine results pages. Amazon will continue to create policies that increase their revenues (such as requiring fees to sell certain brands) and put them first. We expect that down the road Amazon will eventually open the Amazon Vine Program to other third party sellers (again, a fee for use program).

How to get Amazon customer reviews going forward

It is not the end of the world and sellers do still have options to get product reviews. Sellers will need to get more creative. The one thing that all sellers should be doing is utilizing automated email campaigns to reach out to current customers. Programs such as <u>Feedback Genius,</u> Kibly and SalesBacker are great investments that sellers should make if they don't already have them. These programs will send automated email reminders to customers asking for seller feedback or product reviews. The seller creates the emails that go out so this gives the opportunity to test new ideas to drive feedback and reviews.

Another thing that sellers can do is borrow a page from the Kindle Direct Publishing playbook. KDP sellers exchange books for reviews. The exchanges are typically for books at $.99 or free, but this is something that I believe some sellers will implement. Review groups on Facebook may turn into product swap groups, where you find someone with a similarly priced product and exchange product reviews at full price. This is certain a more expensive way to get product reviews, but will give you the social proof you need for your product.

Sellers can also utilize social media advertising to generate sales and potential reviews for their products. This is certainly another costly option for sellers to pursue, but may need to be done to drive the listing traffic they need to rank organically on Amazon. A question we received was if offering something like a "mail-in" rebate redeemable after the purchase and off the Amazon platform could be a way to skirt the rule. These could be considered incentivized Amazon reviews under the new policy and a violation of the updated reviewer guidelines and TOS. It's always better to play within the rules than getting your account banned. The new Amazon review policy effects sellers, but the most creative sellers will find ways to be successful.

Resources

Feedback Genius
An automated email tool that integrates with Amazon to send specific emails to customers at pre-arranged time periods to increase product reviews and seller feedbacks
www.feedbackgenius.com

Salesbacker
Another automated email tool designed to increase your product reviews and seller feedbacks over time
www.salesbacker.com

Kibly
A program partnered with Amazon to automate emails to customers and gain more reviews for your products
www.kifbly.com

THE AMAZON EARLY REVIEWER PROGRAM

A program was announced by Amazon that can help with the entire review process. The Amazon Early Reviewer Program is designed to encourage customers who have already bought a product to leave a review. This program will provide incentives to customers who have purchased a product to consider leaving a review on the product. Amazon's banning of reviews on discounted products has been a huge topic of discussion among sellers, and this program seems like it will be the answer to many of their concerns.

What is the Amazon Early Reviewer Program?

Amazon wants to build increased confidence for customers that the products they are purchasing are good quality. Prior to Amazon banning reviews on discounted products, many sellers and third parties we're manipulating reviews to make their products appear better than they were. Giving away products at a discount for reviews was a huge piece of any product launch strategy. Sellers were concerned that they would no longer be able to get reviews for their product, and that their sales would suffer. The Amazon Early Reviewer Program could be the answer for new products to gain reviews on the Amazon platform.

Amazon will be reaching out to customers who have already purchased the product and ask these customers to share their authentic experience with the product. The idea is that customers will leave honest product reviews and therefore build increased consumer confidence in a product. Unlike Amazon Vine, all customers will be eligible to participate in the program – not just Amazon's top reviewers. The customers selected to review the product will be chosen at random. Customer accounts that have a prior history or leaving abusive or dishonest customer reviewers will be filtered out of the program.

Customers will be encouraged to leave product reviews by being offered Amazon gift cards ranging from $1-$3. The reward is given to customers who leave a review that meet the community guidelines, regardless of whether it is a 1-star or 5-star review. Like the Vine Program, reviews that are part of the Amazon Early Reviewer Program will have a badge that says "Early Reviewer Rewards." Sellers do not have any influence over which customers are select to participate in the program. Assuming the rewards are of enough value to incentivize customers to leave reviews, this could be a huge boost to sellers looking for product reviews. This further increases the importance of the quality of your products and your sales volume.

What We Don't Know Yet

As we mentioned, this program was rolled out and not all the details are available yet. There are a few things that are not entirely clear yet. Amazon has stated that not all products are participating in the Amazon Early Reviewer Program. This could mean that Amazon will be banning products in certain categories from participating in the program, i.e. media. It also could mean that Amazon will not allow all sellers to opt-in based on prior account history or health.

In a similar light, Amazon may only qualify certain products from a seller to participate. Amazon could consider products that have a certain number of reviews already to not be eligible. They may also make products that have had reviews removed for being incentivized ineligible. The announcement indicates that sellers can select products to participate in the program. This could also be an indication that this may be a pay-to-play program from Amazon, and not a free program to sellers across the board. Amazon will continually look for ways to increase their revenue, and we believe almost all sellers will be interested and willing to pay for this program. The Amazon Early Reviewer Program could be a huge boon for sellers concerned with getting reviews for their products.

GROWING YOUR BUSINESS WITHOUT INCENTIVIZED REVIEWS

Amazon is known for its unexpected TOS changes, but this one has been particularly disturbing to sellers. Incentivized reviews, or giving discounted and free products in exchange for reviews on the platform, have been banned. Sellers have enjoyed the practice of encouraging reviews by offering product incentives that entice customers to try their products. This system is not widely utilized by Amazon sellers, but incentivized reviews has been a key tactic for boosting product visibility and brand trust. The good news is that there are still quite a few options available to get the same results. Read on to better understand what this change means for sellers and what can be done to moving forward.

The Ban on Incentivized Reviews

Amazon decided to ban the practice of soliciting reviews for many product types listed on the site. The TOS revisions are very clear. The solicitation of incentivized reviews of any kind is strictly prohibited, whether requested directly or through a review service or other third party that offers similar services. Even implying a connection between a discounted product and a review is considered a violation of the new terms. This therefore means that some promotional and advertising tactics, including placing URLs with affiliate links on product listings, is also disallowed.

Books are exempt from the ban, since Amazon has permitted the release of advance book copies since they started selling them. Reviews that go through Amazon Vine are still allowed, but will be limited to new and pre-release products. Amazon controls the Vine program, so getting a review from that channel entails waiting for Amazon to invite customers to post their reviews.

Amazon released an announcement regarding the update that explains why this change has been made. Amazon refers to its ongoing efforts to make the system of reviews better. To date, Amazon has already penalized thousands of accounts for attempts to manipulate reviews. This TOS change is part of their continuing work to devise stricter review policies that can result in account suspensions even the revocation of Amazon privileges. The company is also working on removing some solicited reviews that that they consider to be excessive, although there has been no comment for clarification on what this term covers.

Apart from Amazon's announcement, analysts have suggested that Amazon has decided to discontinue incentivized reviews for other reasons as well. First, when the news got out that Amazon was allowing sellers to give away products or offer juicy discounts in exchange for reviews, the public's reaction was not all positive. The practice raised a few eyebrows and prompted shoppers to wonder if the stars they were seeing were genuine efforts that stemmed from true satisfaction or because they got a special deal. Press relations were strained for a time after incentivized reviews became public knowledge, and Amazon may have decided to phase out the practice to avoid further damage.

Buyer trust has also been suggested as a main reason why Amazon decided to ban incentivized reviews. Many sellers who are unable to get good reviews on their own approach third party review services. These sellers at times have unrealistic expectations, however, and some have no qualms about employing illegitimate techniques to obtain four- and five-star reviews. A product with high ratings will certainly sell well in the beginning, but if the actual product does not perform as well as the reviews suggest, it will result in a lot of unhappy customers. Because of the hype, their reactions are going to be even worse than if the seller had simply left the product to gather reviews organically and worked on improving it and the systems behind it. In addition, the most diligent customers will most often be able to detect a fake or misleading review, and are likely to share this information with other online shoppers. Reviews are one of the top methods that shoppers use to evaluate products online. When word gets out and buyer trust plummets as a result, it is very bad for a brand. Knowledge of less-than-honest reviews on Amazon can also negatively influence other sellers.

Working Without Incentivized Reviews

Now that we all have a better understanding of the inner workings of incentivized reviews and why Amazon decided that they were bad for business, we can rest a little easier and begin looking towards promoting products in a more natural way.

Don't Stop Running Promotions

Sellers are no longer allowed to tell shoppers that they can get a discount or a free product if they leave a review. Sellers can, however, still give discounts or free products without suggesting that shoppers must leave a review before they can get additional products. Most satisfied customers will leave good reviews if they see that a seller has made an effort to provide them with a quality product and excellent service. Amazon appears to filter out most of the reviews that come from discounted products, however you some do still make it through and the customer can still leave you great seller feedback which will also help your account.

Focus on Better Product Launches

Some sellers spend time planning awesome product launches that they are willing to invest money in. Others will only spend time trying to find ways to do and spend as little as possible. The former certainly take a bigger risk, but will most often end up on top if their product is one to be proud of. The latter will save money over the short term, but will not see much growth down the line. All that it takes to generate an appropriate level of hype is a reasonable investment in optimized listings, a little bit of creativity, and a genuine belief in the product.

Giving promotional discounts and using Sponsored Product Ads as part of a product launch campaign is a good way to get attention early on. It requires additional monetary investment, but can help sellers find the best keywords that they can use to organically optimize their listings after the launch. Sponsored Products is also known to boost organic rankings and tend to cost less the longer they are run. Running Facebook Ads is also a great way to supplement your Amazon advertising.

Optimize Your Product Listings

It will take some time to get your listings in shape, but this should be considered one of the essentials investments that you must make. Take advantage of each feature that Amazon offers to optimize your listings for desktop as well as mobile shoppers. Without incentivized reviews, having an optimized listing is going to play a key role in boosting your product to encourage more sales, better rankings, and more and better reviews.

Maintain a Good Sales Level

Once you get a good level of sales flowing for your quality product, you can expect to get a good number of reviews. Remember to be polite and real when you ask your customers for reviews, focusing first on the customer's experience, making your request a secondary goal. Do not stop your efforts when you get a few good reviews. You need to build a good sales history over several months to be able to maintain high rankings for a longer time.

Give Higher Priority to Customer Communication

Post-sales, a little bit of effort to check in on customers can go a long way to boosting product ratings and higher conversions. As mentioned above, customer communication should never be about asking for reviews but showing a genuine concern for your customers' experience when shopping for your products. Making that effort to reach out to them on a more personal level, especially when they know that you don't have to, will increase their satisfaction levels. Communicating in a professional yet friendly tone can even help you to better manage poor reviews before they happen, and encourage customers to change their bad first impressions.

Once you have made contact and done all you can to keep your customers happy, it will not take much more to politely ask those who have not yet left a review to give their feedback in that form to help other shoppers enjoy the same experience that they have with you. Set up a system for communicating with your customers so that you can reach them in a timely manner to make them feel that you are paying them due attention. If you need to get help to make this possible, consider it a wise investment in your future sales.

Constantly Review and Reevaluate

Amazon is a dynamic platform, and you need to be prepared to go with the flow if you want to become and remain competitive. Here are a few final tips on staying ahead to keep reviews and conversions on an upward trend: First, be prepared to take on the challenge of working without incentivized reviews. Know how many good reviews you need to hit your sales targets and plan accordingly. Second, always begin work on your organic reviews and marketing efforts with your sales targets in mind so that you can maintain the level of income that you want while you adjust to your new strategy. Third, expect that Amazon is going to change things up from time to time, and be ready to make more adjustments to stay on top.

SELLER FEEDBACK ON SELLER CENTRAL

The system for leaving seller feedback on Amazon was purposely created so that shoppers can benefit from the previous experiences of others. Seller feedback is one of three kinds of feedback that customers can leave after making a purchase; the other two being package feedback and a product review.

Seller feedback is important to all third-party sellers since Amazon uses this to gauge the performance of sellers. The customer experience is one of Amazon's top priorities, so they rely on seller feedback to make sure all their sellers are keeping up their end of the bargain regarding product and fulfillment quality, proper packaging, timely delivery, and excellent customer service.

Negative Feedback Rating

Amazon measures a seller's quality through a Negative Feedback Rating. The rating is a percentage of a seller's total feedback ratings, where no more than 5% of a seller's ratings should be negative. Sellers should aim for a score between 0% and 5%, but the closer to 0%, the better. Sellers who get higher negative feedback are advised by Amazon to conduct a review and make the necessary changes to improve customer satisfaction.

Amazon strives to ensure that all their customers maintain trust in the platform. Amazon has grown to be the online retail giant of giants because millions of shoppers leave the platform satisfied. Sellers must meet the following performance targets to secure shoppers' safe experience or risk having their selling privileges revoked:

- Order defect rate: < 1%

- Pre-fulfilment cancel rate: < 2.5%

- Late shipment rate: < 4%

Check Seller Feedback

You can review your seller feedback rating from your Seller Central Account. Navigate to Performance, then to Customer Satisfaction on the dropdown, and click on the Customer Feedback Tab. You will see your star rating above the table, then the positive, neutral, and negative feedback on the table itself. Amazon scores feedback on the following scale:

- 5 stars = Excellent

- 4 stars = Good

- 3 stars = Fair

- 2 stars = Poor

- 1 star = Awful

A rating of 3 is considered a neutral or average rating as far as most customers are concerned. In Amazon's book, however, only 4 and 5 stars are good. 3 is Fair, which for Amazon is on the negative side.

As seen in the list above, seller feedback focuses on rating the quality of the seller based on the criteria of timely delivery, the quality of the product against the product description, and customer service. Responses on delivery, as described and customer service are limited to a Yes or a No, so falling somewhere in the middle has a better chance of getting a negative response. Amazon shoppers have 90 days to leave feedback after making a purchase. After this, you have less than 60 days to resolve any issues so that your customers can remove negative feedback.

Customers' Choice

Getting seller feedback is especially useful to wholesalers and resellers who basically sell the same product. It is how customers differentiate between sellers to choose the one who provides the best product and service.

Buy Box Awarding

Amazon factors great seller feedback ratings into their formula for deciding who gets the Buy Box. Being awarded the buy box increases a seller's chances of being selected by shoppers, so there is a great incentive to pay attention to seller performance. Sellers who fall below the mark have no chance of getting the Buy Box.

Dealing with Negative Seller Feedback

Seller Central Support

Amazon does not usually entertain requests to remove product reviews, but they are open to checking seller feedback. The great thing about the way that seller feedback is managed is that sellers can leave high ratings untouched and have low ratings removed. If you have received feedback that is along the following lines, you can contact Amazon support to ask for it to be removed:

- **includes profanity or obscene language**

- **includes personal or sensitive information such as names and addresses**

- **is a product review instead of seller feedback**

- **the order was fulfilled by Amazon.**

- **involves a problem that is not the seller's responsibility**

- **involves an issue where the order was fulfilled by Amazon – wrong item, late shipment**

To open a ticket with Amazon regarding negative feedback, follow these steps:

1. *Open the Help menu on the top right corner of your Seller Central Account.*

2. *Click on Get support, then Contact Us on the bottom of the pop-up.*

3. *Choose Selling on Amazon, then Customers and orders, and type in the related Order ID.*

4. *Choose the Customer Feedback Removal Request option and click Next.*

5. *If Amazon does not automatically approve the request, you will be directed to select a reason for making the request and to add information that will help your appeal – highly recommended.*

6. *Enter your contact information and send.*

Customer Contact

When your seller feedback is about your performance, Amazon is not likely to approve your removal request. In these cases, you can contact the customer who left the feedback to see if there is anything you can do to change their mind.

From the Feedback Manager dashboard of your Seller Central Account, you can see your Current Feedback. On the list, navigate to the case you want to take care of. You can click Respond, use the Rater Email, or contact your customer directly. The Rater Email is a template created by Amazon, which contains all the basic information. Crafting a personalized email gets better results, however. If you choose this option, locate your buyer's email address on the far right to get started. From the information on the feedback entry, you can offer your apologies, address the customer's comments, offer a solution, and request them to remove the feedback. If all goes well and your customer agrees, you can follow up with these instructions for removing the negative feedback:

1. *Go to http://www.amazon.com/your-account.*

2. *Navigate to the Community column under Personalization and click on Seller Feedback Submitted By You.*

3. *Locate the feedback item that you want to remove and click the Remove link next to it.*

Respond to Negative Feedback

If Amazon does not remove the negative feedback or your customer is unresponsive, you can try to ease its impact by responding publicly. Even if the feedback will remain on your account, you can show that you care about the bad experience and are offering a solution. Most shoppers will check feedback scores just like they check reviews. Your response may not sway all of them back in your favor, but not responding can easily come across as a seller not caring about their customers.

Ask for Positive Feedback

You can also offset negative feedback by increasing positive feedback. It is against Amazon policy to incentivize customers to leave positive feedback, but you can contact customers who have purchased your product to check up on their experience. Express to them that you want to make sure that it was a good experience, and request their feedback.

Using Amazon Seller Central Business Reports to Monitor ASIN Performance

Amazon provides sellers with a lot of advantages, and part of this is all the tools that they have available for use. One of these tools is the "By ASIN" Business reports. Every seller should be take the best advantage of this Amazon-generated report to check on product visibility and sales. Properly analyzing this report will help you as a seller to see not only how your products are faring, but also to see what changes you can make to help them sell better.

What to Check For

By ASIN reporting contains data on the Sessions, Page Views, Buy Box Percentage, Units Ordered and Ordered Product Sales for each of your ASINs. These categories pertain to two general aspects of the products, their visibility on Amazon, and how well they sell.

Analyzing this report from both an advertising and a sales standpoint should become a habit for any seller. When looking at this report for the items below, keep in mind that you are considering the historical performance of your products, their average performance, and the recent changes that are shown. All aspects of ASIN reporting are actionable, but note that some metrics can be dealt with immediately and others will need time to show improvements.

Sessions

Your Sessions column shows how many times each specific ASIN was viewed. Driving traffic to listings is one primary concern that greatly affects sales.

- Low sessions generally mean that your product needs a boost through promotions or paid advertising.

- High sessions and low sales may mean that your listing may need revisions of the content or images, may have poor reviews or not enough reviews to convert, may have a lot of competition that is converting better, or your product does not meet the requirements of Amazon buyers, who can be quite picky.

- Drops in sessions combined with drops in sales usually indicates a problem with the attractiveness of the listing or the product itself

Check on the other criteria as well. Low offer counts and inventory issues can be the reason why your sessions are falling, ow why your products are visible but not flying out the door. Adjusting PPC campaigns, even outside of Amazon, can also affect the performance of your ASINs.

Who's Got the Buy Box

Competitors selling on your top selling listings may be vying for the Buy Box, driving your numbers down. Find out which of your ASINs in the Amazon sales channel are controlling channel performance and how much of the Buy Box (as a percentage) is theirs. This combination is part of a larger strategy that you should consider and fully understand to help your ASINs compete and improve their performance.

Ordered Product Sales

Your Ordered Product Sales show an end-result aspect of how saleable your products are. Very simply, if numbers are going up, your products are selling well, and vice-versa. Ordered Product Sales does not show you the specifics. However, the sales per ASIN and per order, their selling price, and offer count should be tracked in any case, and are easy to compute. You should be looking at the numbers for at least over the past 3, 6 and 12 months. Keep the same record for your Buy Box percentages as well so you can map trends and explore causalities.

True Top Sellers

You may be tracking many top selling products that have given you big numbers over the past several months. The task now is to find your true top sellers by mapping which products have been bringing in the highest revenues over various time periods, and which ones have been topping the chart consistently.

Pay close attentions to those ASINs that are most likely to have a heavy negative impact on your business if performance should take a downturn. Make sure that your efforts are focused on these important ASINs so that they continue to perform well and generate the sales that will fuel your growth.

Top Seller Inventory

Checking inventory is a very important part of making sure that your top sellers continue to perform well. You do not want your optimization efforts, advertising budget – and most importantly your investment in customer trust – to go to waste on products that visitors cannot buy because they are out of stock.

Your inventory should be maintained at levels that will ensure that your top sellers never go out of stock. Zero stock will quickly cause a drop in weekly revenue that can be a huge loss for your business if it is a top seller. Take a quick look at the volume that you are moving for each of these ASINs to show you how much stock you should have on hand for each parent and child.

What to Expect from ASIN Reporting

When you start reviewing ASIN reporting you should be able to gather a lot of insights on the performance of your ASINs. As you dedicate regular time to analyzing the results and implementing different solutions to keep your numbers up, you will see performance steadily improve. As you continually monitor ASIN reporting, you will also find and learn the different nuances that will give you clues into how you can help your products perform even better.

ADVERTISING ON SELLER CENTRAL WITH CAMPAIGN MANAGER

These days, more than half of online shoppers are searching for products directly on Amazon. This is a huge market that no seller would want to miss out on. Amazon advertising is also about 30% more cost-efficient than other online advertising platforms such as Google and Facebook. This is a terrific incentive to start advertising via the Amazon Campaign Manager.

With record numbers of sellers signing on to reap the benefits of Amazon membership, the competition on the platform has surged. Serious sellers must now take their listings a step further, not only optimizing them but also making sure that they are placed where they have the best visibility. Below are the steps for getting started on advertising with the Amazon Campaign Manager to reach more potential customers to boost sales even during slow months.

What is Seller Central Advertising?

Advertising on the Amazon Campaign Manager is available to third-party sellers on the platform. Seller central advertising, better known as Amazon Sponsored Products, are the ads via the Amazon Campaign Manager that place your product listings at the top or bottom of SERPs on the Amazon platform. To make these ads, there is no additional work needed since your listing image is simply resized and the ad headline is taken from your listing title. If your item is in stock and you qualify for the Buy Box, your ad will run over the long term without a hitch.

Amazon Sponsored Products can be Targeted Manually or Automatically.

Manual targeting requires the seller to enter keywords on which Amazon will base matches for your listings to customer searches. With **automatic targeting**, you can leave the details up to Amazon, letting the platform's algorithms show your ads based on all searches that are relevant to your product information. Tracking these ads is also easy with downloadable reports on the terms that customers searched for which led to them clicking on your ads. If you are just starting out with Amazon Campaign Manager advertising, the automatic option can give you great ideas on getting keywords to use down the line. When you have got the hang of it all, you can switch to manual targeting to customize your ads for best performance.

Bidding on Sponsored Products Keywords

Sellers must bid on the keywords that they choose for their Sponsored Products, either using **general terms** for the products that customers are searching or targeting **competitor phrases**. The system is like Google Adwords, so some experience with this and other pay-per click campaigns is very useful. You can use general terms if you are looking for a bigger audience, but targeting keywords that are used by your competitors that you want to beat out will usually bring you better returns. This is especially true if you can show great reviews in comparison to the competition. If you are not in a place where you are ready to go up against the big sellers in your category, a third option is to **cross-sell**. You can divert customers before they see the competition's products by bidding on very popular search terms. You can use a famous product of a big brand, for instance, to capture the attention of your target audience so that they see your listing first.

Setting Up PPC on Amazon Campaign Manager

Access to the Amazon Campaign Manager is a great privilege for sellers when they can use Sponsored Products well. Seller Central advertising can have a significant influence on how quickly and how far you can increase sales. This remains true even if your organic sales have proved highly profitable. So, let's look at how to properly set up Amazon PPC so you can take advantage of the upward track of the ever-expanding platform.

Optimize Your Listing

If you have not already done so, you need to go through your listings and optimize them based on Amazon's newest policies. This includes making the best use of your bullet points, HTML in product listings, adding in your target keywords and using professional images and copy. If you yet don't have at least ten good reviews, we recommend that you work on this before launching your PPC campaigns. Customers might start clicking on your ads like crazy, but they are not going to have much incentive to buy if they can't see proof of how happy others are with your product.

Create a Campaign

1. Open Seller Central and navigate to the Advertising tab next to Orders. Open the Campaign Manager from the drop-down and click Create Campaign.

2. Begin by giving your campaign a name that can be easily distinguished from the many other campaigns that you may be creating in the future. If you can develop a system early on, you will have a much easier time managing all your campaigns down the road.

3. You will want to decide on a daily budget for this campaign next. This will set a cap on how much will go into the campaign, so set it at around fifty dollars if you don't want your ad to get cut off before you can collect adequate data to analyze your conversions. You probably won't be spending nearly that much in the beginning anyway. As your conversions increase,

you will also notice your cost per click decreasing. The next step is setting your target type, as discussed above. If you are trying out Amazon Campaign Manager advertising to get keyword ideas, make sure to take note of all the keywords that Amazon finds for your product so that you can compare them against the phrases that you already have. This may give you additional ideas that you can pick out the new ones that you may never would have thought of on your own.

Start Building Your Ad

When done with the targeting stage, click Next Step. Using a scalable naming convention, name your Ad Group. Then decide on the maximum amount you would like to spend for each click on your ad, and set that as your default bid. You might want to set it relatively high, at around five dollars per click. It is unlikely that you will really be charged that much – it is only to make sure that you don't lose out against other bids.

Keep only the most relevant keywords from Amazon's suggestions and click on Provide Your Own Keywords to add any of your own that you may have found using other tools. Click Add these keywords to enter them.

Make sure that you have not selected an end date for your campaign, review all the other entries, and save your campaign to start running your ad immediately. If you don't want to start just yet, simply pause the campaign as soon as you are redirected to your campaign dashboard. When you are ready to begin gathering the data that you will need to adequately test, start it up and let it ride.

Amazon Campaign Manager

Get ready to boost your return on investment with Amazon's Sponsored Products. Getting into paid advertising on the platform can be an uncomfortable move at first. When you begin to see a change in your conversions and the range of possibilities for re-optimizing your listing for better organic rankings, you will have a better grasp of how Seller central advertising can give you the edge that you need to take your Amazon business to the next level.

USING BULK OPERATIONS TO REFINE AMAZON ADVERTISING CAMPAIGNS

Amazon Sponsored Products are one way that Amazon Seller Central users can boost their product sales. Ads from Sponsored Products show up on the top, bottom and side of search engine results pages and can be identified by the term "Sponsored" above the product listing. Many sellers create advertising campaigns in campaign manager, but do not understand many of the other helpful features within campaign manager. One of these features is Bulk Operations and can be very useful for sellers looking to maximize their Amazon advertising campaigns. Bulk Operations makes creating new campaigns and testing existing campaigns easier, and provides valuable performance metrics.

Creating New Advertising Campaigns

Sellers can create new advertising campaigns quickly with Bulk Operations. To create a new campaign, go to Campaign Manager and click Bulk Operations. You can then download your existing campaign data to an excel file and use that file to create new campaigns, or download a blank template. We would recommend using the blank template to create new campaigns. We have used the downloaded file of existing campaign data to create new campaigns and make changes in the past, and it has not always been accepted by Amazon. Save yourself the hassle and transfer any changes or additions you want to make to the blank template. We have never had any errors when uploading that file.

There are four different types of records in bulk operations: campaign, ad group, ad and keyword. Each of these respective records requires different fields to be filled in on the blank template. The proper way to set up the file is in the descending hierarchy above for each Ad Group.

All record types will need to have a campaign name. Campaigns will need to have a daily budget, start date, targeting type (manual or automatic), and campaign status (enabled, paused, archived). Create single ad groups at a time under a new campaign. The required fields for an ad group are: ad group name (created by you), max bid, and ad group status (enabled, paused, archived). Under your ad groups you will want to list your ads or SKUs that you will be advertising. Populate the ad group name, SKU and status (enabled, paused, archived) columns for all your ads. Finally, the keywords will be added under all the ads. Populate the ad group name, max bid, keyword, match type (broad, phrase, exact, negative exact, negative phrase) and status fields. Repeat these steps for each ad group you want in a campaign, or follow these steps to create new campaigns for each ad group.

Using Bulk Operations Metrics

Bulk operations provides the ability to examine your advertising metrics more in-depth than the campaign manager interface. Campaign manager allows you to view performance metrics in time frames of today, yesterday, week to date, last week, month to date, year to date and lifetime. Bulk operations allows you to pick any specific time frame that you want to look at and download the data into excel for easier analysis. This allows you to look at period to period performance and can better inform you of what changes need to be made to your campaigns.

Improving Amazon Advertising Campaigns with Bulk Operations

The Bulk Operations metrics are very important in testing and improving advertising campaigns. Many sellers think there is a direct correlation between increasing budget spend and increased sales when the reality is that advertising campaigns are much more complicated. The two variables of any campaign are the budget and the bids. The testing you will want to perform depends on what the current state of your campaigns are. If you are not currently maxing out your advertising budget, you will want to start by testing increased keyword bids. Use Bulk Operations to update the keyword bids and let the campaign run for a specified amount of time. We recommend testing over at least a week-long period.

Once you have your new test results for the period, compare them to the prior period where bids were lower. Look at how your advertising spend and sales changed with the increased bid. Consider increasing bids for keywords that had sales improve and decreasing bids where the spend increased and sales did not improve. You can also consider moving better performing ads to new, smaller ad groups where you can focus on using the best converting keywords. This can improve your campaign performance and help you maximize the ROI of your advertising budget.

APPLYING FOR AMAZON BRAND REGISTRY

The single most common recommendation that we make to our Amazon Seller Central clients is to apply for brand registry. Being brand registered with Amazon is the first step that every seller should take toward protecting their brand. It provides many benefits to the seller and allows sellers to pursue other options to protect their brand such as brand gating. Applying for Amazon brand registry is a straight forward process, however there are a few things that Amazon pushes back on. We are going to cover what the Amazon brand registry program is, the benefits of Amazon brand registry and what you need to guarantee your application gets approved.

What is the Amazon Brand Registry Program?

The program was created to give third party sellers more control over their listings on Amazon. Being brand registered makes it easier for a seller to list their products on Amazon and protect their brand. The Amazon Brand Registry Program is open to all sellers and manufacturers who have their own branded products. All private label sellers who mark their products and packaging with their logo are eligible for the program – selling a generic, unmarked product means you are ineligible for the program. Applying for Amazon brand registry has some great benefits that you as a seller need to be taking advantage of.

Amazon Brand Registry Benefits

The Amazon Brand Registry program has incredible benefits for third party sellers. Being brand registered allows you to exert greater influence over the product detail information for your products. Under Amazon's Terms of Service, any third-party seller can sell a product on a listing if the product is an exact match. Counterfeit products and knock offs are against the TOS and Amazon is creating new policies to crack down on these practices, however they cannot catch everyone and may miss some third-party sellers that could be on your listing. Third-party sellers that undercut your pricing to win the buy-box can edit your listing information including the title, bullet points and product description. Registering your brand with Amazon allows you to specify what information about the product is correct and prevents other third-parties from changing the information.

Another benefit of being brand registered is being able to list your products on Amazon using a unique identifier other than UPC or EAN codes. The Global Catalog Identifier (GCID) is assigned to your product based on a key attribute that you select when registering the brand. The key attribute can be a model number or manufacturer part number, for example. The benefit of creating a GCID through Amazon is the cost savings of buying UPC codes. Amazon requires GS1 UPC codes which can be quite expensive (Currently $250 to sign up for 1-10 codes). Sellers with tons of SKUs should consider applying for Amazon brand registry for the cost savings alone.

Amazon created a new policy at the beginning of September 2016 called brand gating. Brand gating provides unique protection for brands selling on Amazon. Being in the Amazon brand registry is an important step in getting your brand gated.

How to Apply for Brand Registry

There are a few things that you should ensure you have done prior to your application. These will save you a lot of headaches down the road and help the process move smoothly. You will need to have a website for your brand, and will need to have an email account hosted on that website. Websites can be built quickly using services such as Wix.com, Squarespace.com, Weebly.com or Wordpress.com, for example. Setting up an email hosted on your domain is also easy. For example, the email should be xxxx@yourbrand.com.

It is also important to ensure that your brand's logo is on both the product and the packaging. You may need to work with your manufacturer to develop new packaging and branding on your product if you currently do not have it. Amazon will not approve an application missing this. Also, ensure the website has images of your product with the logo on the packaging and on the product, itself. Finally, make sure the email hosted on your website is a user on your Amazon Seller Central account.

Here are the steps to register your brand:

1. In your Amazon Seller Central Account, select help and search for Amazon Brand Registry. Click the link that is in Seller Central University

2. On the next page, select "Apply for Brand Registry"

3. Enter your brand name as it is currently listed on your products, upload images of the product and packaging with your brand's logo on it, select "I manufacture the product and own the brand," add in your brand's website and answer the UPC question

4. Click "Submit"

5. Check your Amazon cases to see the status of your request

Following the steps above and the actions to take beforehand will make applying for Amazon brand registry a smooth process. The Amazon Brand Registry benefits will help you as a seller on Amazon. Take the first steps to protecting your brand today.

How to Take Your Brand Global with Amazon FBA

The opportunities for sellers afforded by the Amazon platform continue to appear lucrative. Amazon has had another record fourth quarter in 2016. It's also interesting to see that Amazon Echo and Echo dot we're the best-selling products across Amazon this past year. The popularity and ease of use for the Echo products will continue to lead to increased purchases from consumers on the Amazon platform. While Amazon US will continue to provide incredible opportunities for sellers, our focus for 2017 will be capturing the future growth on the international Amazon platforms. Amazon has made it easier than ever to take your brand global with Amazon FBA.

Selling Internationally on Amazon

There are currently 13 Amazon platforms that you can sell on – from Australia to the United Kingdom. Each platform comes with their own challenges. While these platforms are nowhere as large as the United States, they will continue to grow as Amazon gains popularity in the respective countries. Getting in early and gaining visibility to your product could provide significant long-term growth for your brand. Our recommendation to our clients is to take your brand global with Amazon FBA as soon as possible.

Typical challenges that sellers face include translation & SEO, pricing, and fulfillment. Product sales can also be affected by cultural differences between shoppers. Just because your product does well on Amazon US, does not mean it will perform as strongly in another country. Fulfillment can also be a problem for many sellers. International shipping can be expensive and include numerous taxes and/or transaction fees for those who choose to do merchant fulfillment. However, Amazon FBA is available in the United States, Canada, United Kingdom, Germany, France, Italy, Spain, India and Japan.

Fulfillment Abroad with Amazon FBA

Utilizing Amazon FBA in other countries is the same as it is for the United States. Your products are shipped to the fulfillment center, received and then fulfilled as orders for the products come in. The main differences are with shipping your products to an FBA country different than your own. When you send product to a different country, you are essentially acting as the exporter of record in the product source country and the importer of record in the destination country. We recommend using a freight forwarder to help the process move smoothly. They will know what steps need to be taken and could possibly even have a customs broker as well. We won't cover it in too much detail, but here is a brief overview of the process:

1. Create listings in Seller Central account for the market you intend to sell in

2. Prepare a commercial invoice showing your company as the importer of record

3. Find a customs broker (if your freight forwarder does not have one

4. Ship the products from the factory or warehouse to the port in the source country

5. Get the products cleared through customs

6. Ship the product to the destination country

7. Clear the products through customs in the destination country

8. Have the carrier get the product to the fulfillment center

We believe it is better to let the pros handle those steps. Once your product is processed at the fulfillment center, your products will be live on the Amazon platform.

Amazon FBA European Fulfillment Options

There are a few unique product fulfillment options with Amazon FBA in Europe. Amazon currently offers Unified Accounts in North America and Europe. If you currently sell in the US, you may be familiar with the option to also sell your product in Canada or Mexico. You can use FBA in both countries however all the sales can be managed from a single account. This is the North American Unified Account. You will need a separate European Unified Account, but you will be able to manage your sales in the UK, Germany, France, Spain and Italy from this account. We recommend that you take your brand global with Amazon FBA and the European Unified Account before moving into other markets.

New European Unified Accounts will need to have one of 3 fulfillment options selected: Pan-European FBA, European Fulfillment Network (EFN) or Multi-Country Inventory (MCI).

The most similar option to the United States fulfillment model is Pan-European FBA. Your inventory is sent to a fulfillment center based in one European marketplace and Amazon then distributes it to fulfillment centers in other European marketplaces based on demand (or expected demand). You can avoid per unit fees when shipping products across international borders as Amazon will be doing the distribution across borders. You need to have an active listing on each Amazon marketplace (i.e. .fr, .co.uk, etc.) for your product to be sold in each market under Pan-European FBA. This is by far the most hands off option you can choose in Europe.

The EFN network could be a good option if you expect your products to only be purchased on one European marketplace. Your inventory would be sent to a fulfillment center in one country and the products could be distributed to other fulfillment centers in that country, but not outside of that country. You can still put your products for sale on the other European marketplaces, however you will incur per-unit cross border fees when Amazon ships to locations outside the source country. This could also mean shipped orders could take a few days more to reach customers outside of the source country.

MCI is the final option that you can choose for Amazon FBA in Europe. For MCI, you ship your products to specific marketplaces that you want to sell in. The products are then distributed and fulfilled within that market, but not to other marketplaces. This allows you to keep your inventory in your bestselling locations. It keeps your shipping times low and gets the orders to your customers faster. You are also able to select individual listings that you want to be fulfilled by MCI and do not need to select your entire inventory.

Additional Things to Consider When You Take Your Brand Global with Amazon FBA

We've highlighted how the process works and what you need to know about using FBA internationally, however there are many additional items that need to be addressed. Logistically, you will want to speak with a few freight forwarders or customs brokers to get an idea of who you would like to use and what requirements they have. You should also consider talking to a tax account or tax lawyer who can help you determine what your tax liabilities will be when selling abroad. You may also want to speak with an accountant about how your payments will be received. You can use Amazon Currency Converter for Sellers or set up bank accounts in the individual markets, however each has their own advantages and disadvantages. We are not professional financial or tax advisors and are not in a place to give any tax advice.

There are incredible opportunities out there for sellers looking to go global. As Amazon continues to grow in popularity, sales across the foreign marketplaces will increase. The FBA options provided by Amazon are an amazing way to grow your brand in other markets. While the upside is great, there are also other tax, legal and accounting consequences that you need to consider as well.

UTILIZING ENHANCED BRAND CONTENT

Amazon launched their Enhanced Brand Content feature in a quiet release in November 2016. Enhanced Brand Content gives any third-party seller on the platform who has branded products a new range of product listing optimization options. The Enhanced Brand Content tool is free to use for brand registered sellers, but only for a limited try as part of the test run. It has not been rolled out to all Amazon sellers yet, but we recommend that you try it as soon as it becomes available under your Advertising menu.

Competition on Amazon is becoming increasingly tough. There are now over two million sellers on the platform, and they sold more than two billion products last year. This is stiff competition to face, even for veteran eCommerce retailers. The Enhanced Brand Content feature can give private label sellers a much-needed edge.

Enhanced Brand Content Explained

This A+ Seller Central tool is aimed specifically at boosting conversions for private label brands. Enhanced Brand Content allows sellers to add rich image and text content to their product descriptions. Instead of having a single, plain-text paragraph, Enhanced Brand Content users can add quality images and format their text. This improves description appearances and should fuel additional conversions.

The original Amazon A+ Content feature allowed the addition of HTML premium content. Enhanced Brand Content, however, is available for any branded product that is registered in the Amazon Brand Registry. The feature does not allow fully customized HTML, but its templates offer a lot. Sellers will be able to format text for easy scanning, place emphasis on unique product value points, and include a more comprehensive visual element.

Start Using Enhanced Brand Content

Get Your Products in the Amazon Brand Registry

Your private label brands that have a Global Catalog Identifier (GCID) can be registered quite simply in Amazon's Brand Registry.

Browse the Enhanced Brand Content Feature

The Amazon Enhanced Brand Content page will show up under the Advertising menu once it becomes available on your Seller Central account. The Help section will give you an idea of the basic requirements for creating your Enhanced Content Detail Pages. Prepare your product text and images, and enter your first SKU to begin.

Select an EBC Template

There are five available templates as of now for Enhanced Brand Content; more options than standard A+ Content for Vendors. Each of them has predefined sections for images and text. Here are some features to note when making your selection:

	Images	Text
Template 1	8 images of 300 x 650 pixels maximum	4 placements
Template 2	1 header image of 970 x 600 pixels maximum plus 8 images of 300 x 650 pixels maximum	4 placements
Template 3	2 images of 970 x 600 pixels maximum	2 placements
Template 4	1 header image of 970 x 600 pixels maximum plus 5 images of 300 x 300 pixels maximum	6 placements
Template 5	1 large image of 970 x 1300 pixels maximum	1 placement

It is best to choose a template based on your available images and text. If you have a bit more time and money to spend, you can create new text and design better images to fit your desired layout. If you decide at some point that a different template would be more suitable for your listing, you can easily change it.

Template 1   Template 2   Template 3   Template 4   Template 5

Note also that not every text or image placement must be filled. Any box that is left blank will be automatically adjusted by Amazon to balance out the white space. Images that are very poor quality should be replaced as they can cause your enhanced listing to be rejected. Images that are too large per the above specifications will be automatically resized. Choose a balance between resolution and file size to make the best use of your 250KB size limit for images and text together.

Add Content

Lay out your optimized images and text in the most visually appealing and easy to read arrangement within the template. Remember here that Amazon does not allow the use of any copyright or trademark symbols. Video is also not available for Enhanced Brand Content, but we hope to see this added in the future. Your existing plain text description will be replaced, so make sure that you have all the details in your enhanced placements. One great advantage is that the content can be published to all your ASINs registered in your account's brand registry. If, however, an ASIN has ever had a contribution published by a retail vendor, the content will not be published.

If you are concerned about your m-commerce visibility, you will be pleased to know that there are no additional steps for creating Enhanced Brand Content. It is also adjusted automatically to display on

Mobile or the Amazon App. Not all the images will display, however, until the mobile user clicks on the Description box. Amazon will not index any Enhanced Brand Content, unfortunately, but it does get indexed by Google, so your page will have a higher chance of being picked up by searches if you have properly optimized your listing with relevant keywords.

Preview

Once all your content is in place, you can get a preview of what your enhanced listing will look like. The preview will also bring up warning for any errors such as prohibited references to guarantees, returns, and pricing information. You will need to fix these before your listing can be approved. Finally, you will get a message regarding any available space left, which you should use to add or upgrade images and text. Be sure to remember the limitations placed on image sizes as you do so.

Final Touches

If you see anything that does not look too good, such as odd white space between sections in your layout, check your image sizes and margins to ensure that they fit together seamlessly into your chosen template.

Submit for Review

When you are finished tweaking your listing, you can click on submit. Amazon can take up to seven days to review a listing, but most are either published or rejected within two days. If your listing is rejected, Amazon will provide guidelines for revisions that you can apply to be eligible for resubmission. Visit the Help page as well to brush up on the restrictions. You may get multiple revision requests from Amazon as the listings appear to be reviewed manually. Just continue adjusting your Enhanced Brand Content until the Amazon requirements are satisfied.

Approved

Your listing will be automatically updated by Amazon as soon as it is approved. You can check your new content by visiting your listing. Once you get your first listing approved, you can use this experience to create up to twenty more submissions, the maximum allowed for pending Enhanced Brand Content.

Expanding Beyond Amazon with Multi-Channel Fulfillment

Amazon currently is the largest eCommerce platform and provides incredible opportunities for small sellers and large businesses alike to reach millions of potential customers. The platform has grown, and continues to grow, at incredible rates. Total reliance on one sales channel however will set your business up for failure. We advise and work with our clients to build their Amazon presence, but to also explore setting up new sales channels with eBay, Etsy, Jet or a Shopify webstore. All sellers can easily open new sales channels by using Amazon Multi Channel Fulfillment.

What is Amazon Multi Channel Fulfillment?

The fulfillment by Amazon (FBA) service from Amazon provides sellers the ability to use Amazon to fulfill their orders on other platforms as well. Multi-Channel Fulfillment, as it is known, allows businesses to outsource all their fulfillment to Amazon. Sales that occur on the Amazon platform are automatically fulfilled (as they normally are in FBA), but sellers can submit order fulfillment requests for sales that they have received on other platforms. Amazon charges sellers fees for the shipping & handling. It does not get a referral fee as the sales does not occur on the Amazon platform.

Multi-Channel Fulfillment allows sellers to select standard, expedited or next day shipping options. You can also specify if they want the order to be fulfilled in an Amazon box, or a plain box that does not have any branding. You are responsible for handling all the customer service and returns for orders fulfilled using Amazon Multi Channel Fulfillment.

How do I set up Amazon Multi Channel Fulfillment?

All Amazon FBA sellers are already set up with Amazon Multi Channel Fulfillment as an option. A few fields need to be completed by the seller before they can start using this option. In the Seller Central account, go to settings and select Fulfillment by Amazon. There are many different options on this page. Scroll down to Multi-Channel Fulfillment Settings and select edit. Enter your brand's name in the Packing Slip – Merchant name field. In the Packing Slip – Text field you can type any additional information that you want to give to your customer.

How do I create a fulfillment order with Multi Channel Fulfillment?

Creating fulfillment orders for Multi-Channel Fulfillment is very easy:

1. Go to your inventory page and find the product that needs to be fulfilled.

2. Select "Create fulfillment order." Populate the fields with the information of the customer who ordered the product. Order ID field can be populated or left blank and will be automatically created. You can update the quantity of items being shipped at the bottom of the page.

3. Select continue to advance to the shipping options. There are two options on this page to complete. The first option is the fulfillment action. Select ship this inventory if the payment has already processed and is ready to go. You can select hold if you want to create the order and wait for the payment to complete. Update the status to "Ship this inventory" once the payment is processed.

4. Finally, select the shipping option that you want to use and select "Place Order."

Strategy for Using Amazon Multi Channel Fulfillment

Now that we have discussed what Amazon Multi-Channel Fulfillment is and how to use it, let's talk about some of the strategies you can employ to take advantage of this. The most common way to take advantage of this fulfillment option is to create a Shopify or WooCommerce storefront. Shopify and WooCommerce are easy to use platforms to build an online store for your brand. Creating your own website for sales means that you will need to drive traffic there. The primary ways this will be achieved is through SEO and paid advertising. SEO is a complicated process, but the easiest way to start getting traffic is to install a blog on your store and create social media accounts. Create content for your blog and build a following by connecting with customers who may be interested in your product. Use these customers to create targeted advertising campaigns and drive more potential sales to your page.

A lower cost alternative strategy is to create selling accounts on eBay or Etsy (if your product fits that platform). Listing products on both platforms is an easy process and the fees they take compared to that of Amazon are low. Another great thing is that price arbitrage can exist for your products between these platforms. Prices in one product category on Amazon can be quite low due to competitive offerings or sellers racing to the bottom. You may be able to list and sell your product for higher on a different platform that may not be as competitive.

Using Amazon Multi Channel Fulfillment is a powerful tool to drive additional sales. We believe it is important to diversify your sales channels and have more sources of revenue than just Amazon. The simple strategies that we're highlighted above will be discussed in greater length in the future. Think about how your business would improve through creating new sales channels and start taking advantage of Multi-Channel Fulfillment from Amazon.

Resources

Shopify
One of the fastest growing and most popular eCommerce store front website hosting programs that can be integrated with Amazon accounts to allow customers quick purchases
www.shopify.com

Wordpress
An easy to use interface to build custom stores utilizing WooCommerce or other plug-ins
www.wordpress.org

BigCommerce
An all-in-one eCommerce platform that allows your store to connect Amazon accounts for quick customer purchases
www.bigcommerce.com

STEPS TO DRIVE MORE TRAFFIC TO YOUR SHOPIFY STORE

Creating a successful ecommerce presence involves utilizing as many platforms as possible to reach your audience. Shopify is a great platform to expand your brand's online presence and bring in additional revenue to your business. We've briefly discussed the strategy of building a Shopify store and using Amazon Multi Channel Fulfillment before. We are going to cover ways to drive more traffic to your Shopify store.

The three ways we are going to drive traffic will be through search engine optimization (SEO), social media marketing and affiliate marketing. These play an important role in attracting more shoppers to your website. Following these strategies will set your Shopify store – and your brand – up for long term eCommerce success. It all begins by increasing your online presence!

Increase Your Social Media Presence

Reaching your target audience is simpler than ever thanks to the innumerable social media networks that exist. Your brand needs to have as large a social media presence as possible. It's important to be on the top social media sites for two reasons. Creating social media profiles gives you the opportunity to create links to your Shopify store – which is a huge part of SEO. It is known as link building. The Google search engine indexes your website based on a variety of factors and one of them is the quality of your links. It is important to have links back to your website from "quality" websites. The idea is to get as many links from places like Facebook, Twitter, YouTube, etc. directing people to your website.

Having social media presence on a variety of websites will continue to pay dividends down the road. It will allow you to reach a larger audience and can snowball into additional backlinking to your website. A strong social media presence in combination with the steps below are key as you try to drive more traffic to your Shopify store.

Utilize Facebook Advertising to Better Understand Your Audience

Gaining insight to who your target audience is will be valuable. Facebook advertising provides a great opportunity to collect demographic information on who clicks on your links. Facebook tracks the behaviors and interests of their users. You can obtain that information by creating campaigns on the platform. Facebook ads can be used in a couple different ways. The easiest way to collect the information is to install a Facebook pixel into your Shopify store and create ads directly linking to your website. A Facebook pixel can be used to track different metrics you may be interested in – from page views to conversions. Having a pixel on your website will collect the demographic information as customers visit your site.

Another way you can use Facebook ads is to redirect potential customers to a landing page – either a Facebook landing page or an off-site landing page. The landing page needs to have some type of value proposition to attract shoppers. The value proposition could be a discount or a free eBook on a topic that the shopper gets after entering their email address. Email address collection is the primary goal of using a landing page. The email addresses can be used for advertising campaigns or for email marketing campaigns in the future.

You will be able to collect the demographic information from either method. This demographic information will allow you to create "look-a-like" audiences in the future. This means that the customers you target on Facebook will have similar behaviors and interests to those who previously clicked on your advertisements. You will also use this

THE AMAZON SELLER CENTRAL SELLING GUIDE

demographic information in the next 3 steps as well to drive more traffic to your Shopify store.

Design and Create Content for Your Audience

The demographic data from Facebook will provide great insight to who your audience is. It will provide detailed info on ages, sex, location, interests and behaviors. Your job is to create content that people in those demographics will be interested in. For example, a target audience of 30-49 interested in home appliances may not care much about appliances in new rental units. That audience is typically going to be homeowners and content centered on that topic may not be important to them. On the other hand, content about the top, new appliances that will increase the value of their home could be hugely relevant.

Each audience will be different and you will need to design your content around your audience. Create content that adds value to your target audience and will keep them coming back for more. It's not the quantity of content you put out, but how relevant and valuable it is to your audience. Use the social media profiles you created to distribute the content you create. Install a blog on your Shopify store and post the content there. Ensure the content always has links to your website and other relevant websites. As the content is liked and shared by your audience, more traffic will reach your website and, for SEO purposes, the links to your store will greatly increase.

Content marketing can be a great way to drive more traffic to your Shopify store. It will also be valuable in the next step.

Using Affiliate Marketing Programs to Increase Sales

Creating or enrolling your product in an affiliate marketing program can be a powerful way to get more sales on your Shopify store and increase brand awareness. Affiliate marketing is where you provide commissions for other people to sell your products. Many marketers make their entire living off affiliate marketing and are professionals at what they do. They utilize a variety of techniques like social media marketing, search engine marketing, email marketing and content marketing to reach potential customers. Each affiliate has their own link which records sales that their advertisements get you. You pay them a commission on each sale that they get you. Many times, the content that you have created can also be used by – or improved by – affiliates to drive more traffic to your Shopify store.

Utilizing affiliate marketing may not be for everyone. There are 3 important factors to consider when deciding whether to use affiliate marketers. The first is if your product's pricing allows for enticing commissions for the affiliates. A 50% commission on a $10 product is certainly not as enticing for a 50% commission on a $50 product. The second is if you have the margins to pay an enticing commission. Shopify may allow you to price your products higher than the Amazon platform, but if you're costs are too high you may not make much or any profit from affiliate sales. This is not necessarily a bad thing however. Breaking even on an affiliate sale could make it worthwhile for you. The content they create may increase your brand awareness, drive additional traffic and increases links to your website. It can also increase customer retention for products that may be consumable. The final factor to consider is whether you have inventory or manufacturing capabilities to keep up with the increased sales from affiliates. Running out of inventory costs affiliates money as their advertisements may still be running. This may turn off potential affiliates from working with you.

Utilizing Influencer Marketing to Drive More Traffic to Your Shopify Store

The final step in driving traffic to your website is by reaching out to influencers. Reaching out to topic experts is a great way to get your product more visibility. Experts run blogs, podcasts or social media accounts with large followings. You may be able to get your product featured on their outlet by either sponsoring them, offering the product to them for free or guest blogging for them (great for SEO!). Each expert and what they may be looking for will be different. Trying reaching out to as many as possible to see if there are any opportunities available.

Social media influencers typically have massive followings that are interested in a topic. They typically use the Instagram, Twitter, Facebook or Snapchat platforms to reach people. You can propose having your product featured on their feed when you reach out to them. Influencers will charge you a fee to have the product featured for a certain amount of time, but the fee can be reasonable. In our experience, Instagram is typically where you will find the most reasonable fees. It is important to see what their engagement is relative to their followers. Many pages will buy followers to artificially inflate that number. There are almost unlimited interest pages on Instagram so shop around and find a deal that is right for you.

These 5 steps to drive more traffic to your Shopify store will product incredible results. Some of our clients' stores have been able to achieve over $100,000 in monthly revenue. Growing your brand outside the Amazon platform is key for your long-term success. There are incredible ecommerce opportunities available to those who are willing to put in the work.

Conclusion

At this point you should be aware of how incredibly fast Amazon is growing. The new opportunities afforded by this growth need to be harnessed by every company looking for long-term growth. Amazon will continue to expand and open new avenues to sellers and vendors. Implementing our blueprint or working with us will create a powerful sales channel for your business. We hope our expertise will guide you to success on Amazon.

We've made this book to provide as much information as possible about how we grow our clients' sales. Our blueprint has led to massive growth for our customers, and implementing the same strategies can help you grow as well. This guide will require some testing and experimenting on your part to discover what strategies work the best for your business. Expect that you will face failures or obstacles as you begin to refine and harness the power of these strategies. Do not quit on these strategies quickly when these challenges arise. Use them as opportunities to grow, expand upon and refine our advice to work for you.

We hope that you have enjoyed learning more about the Amazon platform and our blueprint for success. The opportunity to grow on, and with, the Amazon platform are almost unlimited. Our hope is that these strategies change the course of your company and business forever. Thank you for giving us the opportunity to help you realize your brand's eCommerce potential.

We understand that implementing many of the strategies in this book may be a challenge for business owners to focus on. We strongly believe that focusing on your strengths and finding others to compliment your weaknesses is the best way to grow. If you need help implementing any of the strategies that we have mentioned in this book, please reach out to us at www.amzadvisers.com. Take advantage of what you have learned and take your business to the next level on Amazon today!

LIST OF RESOURCES

Google Keyword Planner
Free keyword research tool that can provide valuable insight to high traffic keywords on the Google Search Engine
www.adwords.google.com/KeywordPlanner

Keyword Inspector
A keyword research tool developed for Amazon sellers that focuses on finding the keywords that customers use while searching for a product or niche
www.keywordinspector.com

Sellics
A suite of tools that offers a free trial and is designed to help research keywords, optimize listings and grow your business
www.sellics.com

Jungle Scout
A powerful research tool that extrapolates Amazon marketplace data to provide insights into monthly sales, revenue and best seller rankings based on keyword searches
www.junglescout.com

AMZ Tracker
A suite of tools to help you research products, track competitors and optimize your listings
www.amztracker.com

Feedback Genius
An automated email tool that integrates with Amazon to send specific emails to customers at pre-arranged time periods to increase product

reviews and seller feedbacks
www.feedbackgenius.com

Salesbacker
Another automated email tool designed to increase your product reviews and seller feedbacks over time
www.salesbacker.com

Kibly
A program partnered with Amazon to automate emails to customers and gain more reviews for your products
www.kibly.com

Shopify
One of the fastest growing and most popular eCommerce store front website hosting programs that can be integrated with Amazon accounts to allow customers quick purchases
www.shopify.com

Wordpress
An easy to use interface to build custom stores utilizing WooCommerce or other plug-ins
www.wordpress.org

BigCommerce
An all-in-one eCommerce platform that allows your store to connect Amazon accounts for quick customer purchases
www.bigcommerce.com

Freeeup
An outsourcing business that has affordable, highly skilled workers to help you focus on growing your business
www.freeeup.com

Upwork
A website for freelancers with all types of skills that can help you affordably outsource work
www.upwork.com

TaxJar
A program that integrates with Amazon and tracks all the sales tax that you are required to pay for each sale on the platform
www.taxjar.com

Printed in Great Britain
by Amazon